Geoffrey Boycott was born in Yorkshire in 1940, and made his first-class debut for the county in 1962. Two years later he made his first appearance for England and went on to play 108 Tests for his country, scoring a then-record 8114 runs, including 22 centuries. His career total of 48,426 first-class runs is the most by any batsman since the Second World War. After retiring from the game in 1986, he has gone on to have a second career as a hugely respected broadcaster and commentator. In 2012 and 2013, he was president of Yorkshire CCC. He lives in Yorkshire and in the Cape Province in South Africa, with his wife Rachael. They have a daughter, Emma.

Nick Hoult, who worked with Geoffrey Boycott on the writing of this book, is the deputy cricket correspondent for the *Daily Telegraph* and has covered the sport for more than 17 years for various newspapers and magazines.

THE CORRIDOR
OF CERTAINTY

Geoffrey Boycott

SIMON &
SCHUSTER

London · New York · Sydney · Toronto · New Delhi

A CBS COMPANY

First published in Great Britain by Simon & Schuster UK Ltd, 2014
This paperback edition published by Simon & Schuster UK Ltd, 2015
A CBS COMPANY

1 3 5 7 9 10 8 6 4 2

Simon & Schuster UK Ltd
1ˢᵗ Floor
222 Gray's Inn Road
London WC1X 8HB

www.simonandschuster.co.uk

Simon & Schuster Australia, Sydney
Simon & Schuster India, New Delhi

A CIP catalogue copy for this book
is available from the British Library.

ISBN: 978-1-47113-004-5
eBook ISBN: 978-1-47113-003-8

Typeset in the UK by M Rules
Printed and bound by CPI Group (UK) Ltd, Croydon, CR0 4YY

CONTENTS

INTRODUCTION

Over the years I have written lots of books about cricket but just one autobiography, which was published in 1987. That book was dominated by cricket, because I saw my life purely as a cricketer. Since then I have been asked on numerous occasions to bring my life up to date, however this book is neither just about cricket nor an autobiography – it's a bit of both, covering my recollections of the past, views on the present, righting some wrongs and discussing the issues that are important to me.

For the first time I have 'opened up' about my personal life, something in the past I guarded with the same passion I put into batting, and reflected on how fatherhood altered my priorities.

It has taken more than 11 years for me to be ready to recount the terrifying and painful months spent facing the greatest battle of my life. I was diagnosed with cancer of the tongue on 4 September 2002 and told I would be dead within three months if I did not embark on a gruelling round of treatments. I have been honest about that experience and held nothing back. Even after all this time, it surprised me how emotive and distressing it was to recall the horrific impact those treatments had on my body. It is not what the cancer does to you, but the torture you have to put yourself through to be cured, and the fact that even then, at the back of your mind, you are thinking: 'I might go through all this and still not survive.'

In the darkest moments, I drew on some of my cricketing experiences to help pull me through. I would count off my sessions of radiation with the same determination I counted my runs on the way to scoring another hundred. But unlike cricket, where I reached the top solely down to my own efforts, cancer was not a one-man battle. This time I couldn't have done it on my own. Without the support and bullying encouragement of my wife Rachael, I would not be here now. She has also helped me fill in some of the gaps, parts I had presumably forgotten because I was either too ill at the time to take it in or I had blacked them out as they were too painful to recall.

Rachael and I also wanted to show that dealing with cancer is not just about the person afflicted, it hurts loved ones just as much, as they face the awful task of nursing the sufferer through their treatment, while dealing with their own feelings of fear and despair.

I hope by committing my cancer story to paper it may be of help to anyone who is unlucky enough to be diagnosed with this awful disease. I can understand why some people give up and decide they have had enough, but all I can say is you need a positive outlook and the courage to complete the treatment. That's all you can do; it's what I did, and I am delighted to be here to tell that story.

Such an experience changes your outlook on life and this book is certainly not just about fighting cancer. I've never written before about how I repaired my relationship with Fred

Trueman, and I wanted to try to show the real Brian Clough, two of the greatest characters in British sporting history. Cloughie loved his cricket and was one of my best friends. He was a manager who conquered Europe, not once but twice, with great football and an infectious personality. Sadly, many of the modern generation remember him only as the alcoholic wreck portrayed in the film and book, *The Damned United*.

It is more than 30 years since I last opened the batting for England and my final appearance for Yorkshire was at Scarborough on 12 September 1986. I have never picked up a cricket bat since, not even for charity. I don't want to play if it cannot be at the top. But on that September day, when I walked off the field at 5.21pm, the saddest thing of all for me was that neither the Yorkshire members, the press nor even I knew it was to be my last match. There was no fanfare, no applause, no plaudits.

After playing for the club for 25 years, in 414 matches and scoring 32,570 runs, the ex-players on the Yorkshire cricket committee were so bitter and resentful of my rapport with the members that they deliberately held back their decision it would be my last season. True to form, they gave no thought for anyone else and did not allow my Yorkshire supporters a chance to say goodbye and thank you; nor was there an opportunity for me to thank them. I feel it was a wicked thing to do. In this book I recount my recollections and battles with these committee men, and how I retaliated after some of the old enemies and jealousies resurfaced when I became the club's president in 2012.

But this isn't just a case of me trying to answer my critics. I know I have made mistakes in my life, and growing older has given me a new perspective on events, so I wanted to explore some of those mistakes and assess what I did wrong. I now realise that taking on the captaincy of Yorkshire, and not playing for England for three years, was one of my greatest cricketing regrets.

Listening to Tony Greig's widow at his memorial service prompted me to reflect on one of the great myths of cricket: the Packer series, which so many believe changed the face of the game. I was at the heart of it, and one of only a few left who really knows what went on, so I wanted to set the record straight on this subject that continues to cause debate even now.

Cricket is all I have known for more than 50 years and I have been fortunate to have made two very successful careers out of it. My commentary job takes me all over the world and I have seen at first hand the problems the game faces. The greatest by far is the horrible, modern scourge of sledging, which is dragging cricket down, and our administrators are too weak to do anything about it. I would have no problem dealing with the sledgers!

Of more immediate concern is the state of this England team. Why did Kevin Pietersen's career have to end? How did Australia win the Ashes 5–0 and just what can England do to win back the urn?

These are some of the issues from the past, present and future that interest me, and I hope this book captures them all, for one thing that has never changed is my love for the game of cricket.

Geoffrey Boycott
Boston Spa, Yorkshire
May 2014

CHAPTER I

TROUBLE AND STRIFE

Throughout my cricketing life I have made enemies and I accept it has often been caused by my forthright character, which has sometimes rubbed people up the wrong way. For that I am sorry.

My mother used to say I had tunnel vision. I can hear her now: 'Our Geoff has got blinkers on; he just sees what he wants and goes for it.' She knew from personal experience what I could be like. I once passed Mum in the street near our house and did not even speak to her because I was so deep in thought about my knock earlier that day. She was mortified and in tears when I got home, but I was just thinking about my batting and unable to see the world around me.

I agree that my single-minded approach was a failing in life, but if I upset people it was never intentional – it was just the unfortunate result of a burning desire to get the best out of myself and achieve as much as possible. I did not find it easy to get to the top: I had to fight hard, make the most of my talent and believe in myself. Throughout my teens and early years, people were always telling me I was not good enough and that I would never make it as a cricketer. So, looking back, I think that made me develop a hard outer shell to keep going and stay focused on my goal. This thick skin helped me cope with rejection and gave me the confidence to ignore the doubters, but perhaps it had its downside as well.

During the 1980s, Yorkshire Television ran a programme on which a personality would have their handwriting, palm and horoscopes read. The experts did not know the identity of the person they were assessing, and I remember how the palmist said I was 'an introvert extrovert'. I was somewhat baffled by this description, but Rachael said it summed me up perfectly. She had seen me in new situations appearing to be full of bravado, when she knew that really I was so unsure of myself.

When it came to cricket, there was much less debate about my personality: I was a perfectionist, always striving and never satisfied from the day I started until I retired. When batting, I would shut out all the noise of the crowd, the chirping from other players and just be in my own world concentrating on the ball. Even now, when I play golf, it is impossible to put me off. I still have the ability to shut out all extraneous noise, so if you clap or shout at the top of my backswing or when I'm putting, it doesn't affect my concentration. It is the result of a life spent completely focused on the end goal.

It was reinforced early in my international career when I met the great tennis player Fred Perry. It was early in 1968 and I was a junior member of England's tour squad to the West

Indies. On a drive from Kingston to Montego Bay in Jamaica, we stopped off at a place called the Runaway Bay Hotel. Fred was in charge of the carts at the golf course, hiring them out to the mostly American guests. I was amazed when he came over to talk to me. I was not the star – Colin Cowdrey, Ken Barrington and Tom Graveney were the senior players – but he wanted to talk to me because he said he enjoyed watching my batting.

I would be lying if I said I can remember verbatim what he said to me all these years later, but the general message remains clear in my mind. He told me I had to be focused on myself if I wanted to reach the top and warned me that it can be a lonely, long journey, however if I wanted to be the best I had to have a selfish mindset. He was right. Look at Nick Faldo, who has been compared to me in terms of his character and single-minded approach to his sport. We both had this all-consuming desire to be number one at what we did. What I've learned now is that it is okay to have that mindset, but it should never be to the detriment of others.

It was because of this that I always knew during my career that I did not want the commitment of marriage and children, thinking it would be impossible to do justice to my cricket along with taking on the role of a husband and father. As a professional cricketer, I needed the freedom to go and travel whenever and wherever my job took me.

I met Rachael Swinglehurst on 6 September 1974 at the Lamb Inn, Rainton, near Ripon. Yorkshire had awarded me a benefit that year, and the landlord of the pub organised an event in my honour. I can still remember what she was wearing when we first met, but did not know at the time that it was to be the start of a 40-year, on-off love affair, and she would become the mother of my only child and eventually my wife.

In those days, international tours lasted much longer than they do nowadays. and Rachael would join me when her job allowed, but after our daughter Emma was born in 1988 she was no longer as free to do that.

Rachael was living with her parents near Whitby when the press somehow found out about Emma's birth and, unbeknown to anyone, got a photograph of the little one, aged about six months and printed it on the front page of the *News of the World*. After that they did some despicable things to try to get Rachael to talk, even threatening to print a story that her brother was the father so it must be a case of incest, which eventually forced her to issue a statement confirming I was Emma's father. They even offered her six-figure sums, which is a lot of money now, never mind then, for a kiss-and-tell story, but she wouldn't do it.

From then on, the press were quite relentless in trying to get any information they could about her and Emma, as all my cricketing career I had fiercely guarded my private life from the papers. Rachael hated being constantly followed, so when Emma was nearly two years old, and her parents moved to Tenerife, she decided to go too, and they lived there for a few years.

However, both Rachael and I thought it important that Emma be schooled in England. So when circumstances brought us back together in 1996, my daughter was nearly eight before I first started to get to know her. However, it was not for another three years until she and Rachael came to live with me permanently at my house in Woolley. Wow, that was an awakening!

Suddenly I had this child in my house, someone who took no prisoners – a mini-me, if you like. All my adult life, for differing reasons, I had been indulged by those close to me without fully appreciating it, but not anymore. Emma wasn't bothered about the fact I was a 'celebrity', held in high esteem by millions of cricket fans around the world. As far as she was concerned, I was just her dad, and she believed that role should take priority over anything else.

I was nearly 60 years old and, for the first time in my life, there was this little mite telling me my duties. Sometimes when she asked me to do something, I would say: 'But what if I don't want to do that?' In her mind, it was simple: 'You have to, you're my father.'

Things changed in so many ways. I would be standing at the toilet in the bathroom and she would walk in. I would tell her: 'I'm having a wee,' but her reply would be: 'So, I need to talk to you.' This was totally new territory for me, and it took some getting used to, but I tell her now I wish I'd had three like her. Emma and Rachael both made me realise there is more to being on the planet than cricket and worrying about yourself.

People think it was getting cancer that changed me, and it did. When you fear time is limited, your priorities do change, but it really started a few years before that. Close friends tell me I had become a lot more mellow once my two 'girls' had become my life.

Their influence changed my perception of others, and Rachael played a large part in healing a rift with Fred Trueman. One of my greatest regrets is that I spent 18 years without him in my life. From 1983 to 2001 I had no direct contact whatsoever with Fred, even though we never actually had a cross word. It pains me now to think about all those wasted years not hearing Fred's anecdotes or being around such a unique personality. He was the 'greatest living Yorkshireman', and proof of his legacy is the fact you only have to begin a story with 'Fred' or 'FST' and people know instantly who you are talking about.

I told Rachael and Emma that I idolised Fred from the age of 11, when I went to Headingley for the first time to watch international cricket and saw his Test debut in 1952. In the second innings, India were reduced to 0 for four and bloody terrified of facing Fred, who picked up three wickets in his first eight balls. He had the most perfect action and even now I still marvel over it: sideways on at delivery, looking through the left arm, with a lovely glide to the crease. He was so poised at delivery, it was a thing of beauty watching him run up and bowl the ball.

I first met him in person at the Yorkshire nets in around 1956. By then I was a teenager playing for Barnsley alongside Michael Parkinson and Dickie Bird, and I was invited to practise with the senior players, which was how they judged young cricketers in those days. We did not have purpose-built nets at the time, and instead we had to use the old tea room, which had poor lighting, an uneven surface and of course we had very little protective gear. Fred bowled quickly at everyone – that was his way.

I only found out many years later, after scoring my 100th hundred in 1977, that Fred was asked to give his verdict on me in the nets. He told the BBC in an interview that Arthur Mitchell, the tough old goat who was head coach, asked him to bowl flat out at this 'young 'un'. Fred said he saw this weedy-looking young kid with glasses and a cap on and said: 'Are you sure?' Mitchell replied: 'Ay get stuck in to the little bugger.' After 20 minutes in the nets, he asked Fred for his verdict.

Fred told him: 'He's got a fucking good defence, not easy to get him out, but doesn't have any shots.'

Mitchell said: 'Ay, but just think how good he'll be when we teach 'im to play a few shots.'

It was a great experience to face Fred at that age, and it also meant I was no longer quite so in awe of him when I played alongside him in the first team. It was lovely being on the same side, because it meant I could take the mickey out of him and not worry about having to face his bowling later. Eventually he got his own back, though. We had pre-season nets in Bradford one year and the pitches were wet through and pretty lively. Fred bowled quickly and kept hitting me on the gloves, when I came out of the nets I had bruised hands and the skin on my fingers was ripped off. He came up to me and said: 'I told you I'd get you, you four-eyed little bugger.' He had a long memory.

Of course one of his famous methods to unsettle opponents would be to go into their dressing room before play and pick his targets. Some enjoyed it and looked forward to it happening, others tried every trick in the book to keep him out. Jack Bannister, who had a long career with Warwickshire, tells a lovely story about how they locked the door of their dressing room to keep Fred out before a game in Bradford in the 1960s.

Fred was on 91 wickets in the middle of July and wanted nine more to be the first bowler in the country to reach 100 wickets. 'The first rattle of the door-knob came at 10.30am, followed by five others in the next 35 minutes, before a seventh was accompanied by a voice saying: "Tea lady here with your tea and biscuits." The door was opened and in she came with FS just behind. He stood there like John Wayne entering a hostile Wild West saloon and then delivered his crushing remark: "Right, you lot. I want nine for a hundred, so you can draw lots for who is the odd one out."'

Priceless! You can see why I missed Fred for so many years.

At the heart of our fallout, and so many others in my life, was Yorkshire cricket. When I was sacked as a player in 1983, it tore the club apart. The members rose up and voted to sack the committee and reinstate me as a player. It has been well documented before, so I do not need to go into it again in detail, apart from to place it in the context of my relationship with Fred.

He was on the cricket committee which recommended they sack me at the end of the season. Yorkshire had just won the Sunday League under Ray Illingworth, who was captain and manager, and I had played in 13 of the 16 matches. The club had awarded me a testimonial in 1984 for 20 years' service, so I thought I was in their plans. I had also performed pretty well in the Championship, so sacking me was always going to be a hard sell to the general committee, which was not made up of ex-players.

The thing people always have to keep in mind about Yorkshire cricket is that we are a members' club. It is one member, one vote, regardless of how rich or poor you are, or how many runs or wickets you have to your name. This was something those past players, who had started all the trouble, had forgotten. When the cricket committee did manage to persuade the general committee round to their way of thinking, all hell broke loose. The members forced a special meeting in

Harrogate on 21 January 1984. There were three resolutions: firstly to give Geoffrey Boycott a contract, secondly a vote of no confidence in the cricket committee and thirdly a vote of no confidence in the general committee. All the motions were passed, and the following day both committees had to stand down and hold new elections.

I am not egotistical about it; they did not lose their jobs only because of me. I was just the last straw and the members had seen enough of autocratic committeemen sacking the club's great players. They had sacked Brian Close, forced out Ray Illingworth and even going back to the 1950s they had sacked Johnny Wardle.

It was time to listen to the people, and Fred was now on thin ice. He'd been the most vocal and high profile in trying to persuade the members to back my sacking. There was no doubt that he was chosen to be their spokesman because of his tremendous record and standing in Yorkshire cricket. But then Fred decided to make his biggest mistake: full of bluff and bluster, he announced he would stand for re-election on an anti-Boycott ticket. He promised that if elected he would vote again for me to be sacked. I think he assumed his name and legendary status would guarantee him votes, but it did not. He lost in his ward to a local man who I had never met, a printer named Peter Fretwell, and it was humiliating.

It was amazing to see such an iconic player rejected, and from then on he held me responsible for this embarrassment. This is what Yorkshire cricket does to people; it can be so emotional and irrational. All of Fred's decisions and choices in this controversy were made by him, not me, but he now saw it as my fault that he had lost his seat on the committee. He was very bitter about the whole thing, and from then on no longer went anywhere near the club. He felt betrayed and angry, but what he failed to understand was that the members voted against him not because of his great deeds for Yorkshire but because they felt he had let them down by ignoring their wishes.

After that whenever he gave an after-dinner speech, it seemed he would take any opportunity to rubbish me and lampoon my character. I suffered in silence for years as Fred bad-mouthed me to anyone who would listen, and all contact between us ceased completely. I never once rubbished him and still fondly remembered this great character and bowler. Fred had fallen out with me, not I with him.

Quite a time after everything had happened, I heard Fred on the radio saying that supporters of mine at the time had sent him hate letters and made abusive phone calls, which had upset his wife greatly. Once again, by association I was getting the blame, but in fact I had known nothing about such things, and it was most definitely not something I would have agreed to. I immediately wrote to his wife, Veronica, to explain this to her and to say how sad and sorry I was it had happened. I never received a reply.

Sometime around 2000, I was not writing for a newspaper and was approached to take over Fred's role at the *Sunday People*. I was told that the paper was going to 'retire' Fred as their cricket correspondent. I asked if he knew about this retirement, and was told 'not yet'. While I would have welcomed the job, I decided to turn it down as I did not want Fred blaming me for losing him his job.

By that stage, I was living with Rachael and Emma, and they

would often hear me telling funny stories about Fred, and how I understood why he was angry with me but thought it was irrational and unfair. Rachael is much better at handling people than me. She has a warm personality and is smart at building bridges, so in 2001 she noticed Fred's 70th birthday was looming and persuaded me to send him a birthday card.

I was reluctant at first, because I did not want this gesture thrown back in my face. I thought: 'What is the point? He will only chuck it in the waste paper basket and ignore it the same way my letter to Veronica had gone unanswered years before.' But Rachael chivvied me along, bought a card and I sat down to write it. Obviously, I do not have a copy, but basically I poured it all out, describing him as the greatest living Yorkshireman, as a fast bowler up there with the best ever and recalling how I had admired him ever since his Test debut. I finished by telling him he was a legend in his lifetime.

No reply was forthcoming, but not long after a friend told me Fred's attitude to me had totally changed. He said Fred had been touched by my gesture and immediately taken any nasty or negative things about me out of his after-dinner speeches. A year and a half later, I was diagnosed with cancer and our friendship was rekindled. After I recovered, he and Veronica came to parties at Woolley on a few occasions. Fred would regale all the guests with his lovely stories and jokes. Rachael and I got invited back to their house once for lunch. I even finally persuaded him to start coming to matches at Headingley again after nearly 20 years away.

But think of all those wasted years, all over a row about Yorkshire cricket. I try not to dwell on those bad times, I now just concentrate on Fred the character and Fred the bowler.

During a Test match at Lord's when there had been a rain delay, Michael Atherton once asked me how good he was. During the break, old black and white footage had been shown of Fred bowling in his pomp. These old grainy images always slow down the action, but what I said to Michael was: 'Listen, how good do you think Waqar Younis was? Fred had the same pace as Waqar at his best, but unlike Waqar he could swing it out and cut it back off the seam. He had an outswinging yorker that was lethal. That gives you some idea of how good FST was.'

When I was invited on the Yorkshire board in 2004, I proposed that we nominated some of our former great players for president and put forward Fred's name, which was seconded by the chairman Colin Graves, but sadly we were outvoted three to two. Robin Smith, the deputy chairman, felt it should go to Bob Appleyard instead, so he was made president for 2005 and 2006.

Fred died in the July of Bob's second year, so sadly by the time the position became vacant again, FST was no longer with us. Happily, I did manage to get the board to name something after Fred. I wanted it to be one of the stands at Headingley, but had to settle for an enclosure behind the bowler's arm. Again the saddest thing is he never got to witness and enjoy that either – why do people have to be dead before they get recognised?

I shake my head when I think of the pain caused by Yorkshire cricket down the years and, unlike my relationship with Fred, one of those rifts will never repair.

When the possibility had been mooted in 2010 that I might be nominated by the board for the presidency, unfortunately the old rivalries and problems of the past resurfaced. Two former players came out of the woodwork to raise strong objections. Richard Hutton led the way, but Bob Appleyard later joined him in a bid to stop my taking up the role. For more than 25 years, these two, along with Bob Platt (a big pal of Fred's), appeared to hate me with a passion, and word would often get back to me of some of the things they had said about me. If ever I was in the same room as them, they seemed to avoid making eye contact, and would stand in a huddle whispering to each other.

Hutton disliked me as soon as I became captain of Yorkshire in 1971, and appeared to resent the fact that I was leading the club, an achievement he failed to match. Richard is bitter and I felt had an obsession with me. I have never trashed his cricket ability, and always picked him in my side when I was captain, because he was a good county cricketer, and I respected and admired his father, Leonard's, performances. Len was one of the all-time great batsmen, the first professional to lead England and an Ashes-winning captain. He was loved by the public, but as can often happen his son struggled to live up to the family name.

Richard could never match his father's abilities as a cricketer, but he could have established his own legacy by becoming captain of Yorkshire, a feat that eluded Len, but his chances ended when I got the job ahead of him. I think he has been frustrated about this missed opportunity ever since; indeed, even when we were playing on the same team, I gathered that he made it clear in the dressing room that he was not sorry to see me get out.

Just before it was announced that I was going to be nominated for the 2012–13 presidency, I was in Australia commentating on the Ashes tour and our chairman, Colin Graves, told me the club had received a letter from Richard explaining why I was most unsuitable to be president. Colin and Robin Smith went to see Hutton to try to placate him and to talk him out of continuing in this vein. They even offered to put him forward for a vice-presidency, which he accepted, but he was still not for turning, and fortunately for me, neither were the board.

His letter, sent in November 2010, started with him explaining how he was a past player and came from a family that had 80 years' association with the club. He went on to say: 'The bestowal of the presidency is a considerable honour; of which I do not think Mr Boycott is worthy. His contractual disputes during his playing days brought the club to its knees more than once and damaged its standing and reputation with a wider public. The legacy still stands. Mr Boycott continues to be a controversial and divisive figure. My experience of him is that he is self-seeking and self-serving. There are too many stains on his character for his being the true uniting force that the club should be seeking in its president.'

He carried on with some drivel about the fact I lived in Jersey, which was bound to affect the time I could give to the job, and my refusing to join the Yorkshire past players' association. He even mentioned my unwillingness to help some guy I had never heard of who was writing a book about past players. Apparently, according to him, this showed how disassociated I was with all at Yorkshire cricket. He finished with a flourish saying there was 'considerable and growing' opposition against my becoming president and he 'feared' that some might go public, plunging the club into a 'new dark age'. He concluded by suggesting he would be pleased to meet up and advise the committee in finding a more suitable candidate.

Wow! The same old pompous, superior attitude remained. I thought it was a load of old rubbish. He was still raking over the past, and I pondered for quite a while if I should just ignore it or not. I'd had years of him sniping about me, but this was in a new league. This was a nasty thing to do. To have sent a letter like this to me would have been one thing, but to send it to my chairman and colleague on the Yorkshire board was out of order.

Rachael was as upset by this as I was and said that I should reply. We knew it was not going to change his attitude, but thought that it was time to stop turning the other cheek and give like for like. So I sent a letter to him in June 2011, itemising my response to everything he had brought up.

I began by saying: 'Your misguided self-importance is unbelievable, the more so as you're not even a member. Where were you for the club after your retirement in 1974 to now?' I pointed out that, unlike him, I had been a paying member since 1973, even while playing for the club and only stopped when, with the members' approval, I had been made an honorary life member in 1993. Given that Richard had moved down south, got a job with his wife's father; despite this, it hadn't worked out and he returned to Yorkshire only a few years previously, I told him it was disingenuous to suggest where I lived had anything to do with how I would carry out the role. Furthermore, he knew nothing of my future plans (we had in fact already decided to move back to Yorkshire and were looking for a house).

As regards the past players' association, I pointed out these get-togethers were supposed to be enjoyable, and that wasn't going to happen for me when he and his cronies did nothing but 'slag me off' and could not even bring themselves to acknowledge me. I described his comments about my past contractual disputes with the club as 'a load of tripe', adding that 'the only people who believe that are ones with ulterior motives, who want it to be so, like you; the disputes were about me, but not of my making. I did not sack myself and did nothing to justify such action.' I told him he was being condescending to the members of the time who rose up in revolt.

I pointed out my name, through my own efforts as a player, member, committee man and board member, had been associated with YCCC for nearly 50 years. During that period, I had latterly not received any expenses for my time and in addition had raised a lot of money speaking at events for them free of charge.

On a more personal level, I said he had been hostile to me for years. 'Your father was loved, respected and admired by many people around the world, but particularly in Yorkshire. So many doors have opened to you and opportunities have been given to you because of your father. You have ridden on his coat tails most of your life. It is his name and his achievements – not yours – that give you entry to so many things. All this negativity is both harmful to me and Yorkshire cricket, but quite frankly it does you the most harm. Isn't it time it stopped?' Needless to say, I did not get a reply and am delighted that Richard Hutton never came near the club during my presidency.

Not long after the Hutton episode, Bob Appleyard wrote to

the chairman opening up a different old wound. Bob and I respected each other for our cricketing achievements, but we clashed in the late 1980s, while both elected committee men, over the future of Yorkshire's cricket academy. It was he who had the original idea of an academy; he developed it and deserves all the plaudits for many of the fine players we have produced since its inception. I believe it is the best finishing school in the country, and there are plenty of players in the England side who have benefited from the skills of our coaching staff. Whenever I speak on this subject, I give Bob credit for establishing an academy in the 1990s. But although we agreed over the principles, there was one issue where we differed: where it should be based.

Bob is a Bradford man and at the time the committee also had quite a few other people from the same area. They wanted the academy to be separate from Headingley and suggested it should be established at Bradford Park Avenue, which had been closed for some time and had become derelict. I think Bob hoped moving the academy there would bring investment to the ground, with the view that Yorkshire would eventually return and play championship matches there once again.

I thought that the cost of such an operation was crazy and I pointed this out at committee level. I did not understand why we would want an academy miles away from the club's home. At Headingley we had all the facilities, but if we set up in Bradford we would have had to buy new equipment and spend thousands upgrading and staffing the premises. Although Bob had managed to persuade some local businessmen to sponsor some of the running costs every year, I felt that could not last and that Yorkshire would still have to make up the shortfall –

it was money we could not afford. Regrettably, I was out-voted by the Bradford contingent.

Ten years later, in 1999, the accountants told us the academy would have to close, as it had cost the club in total around an extra £170,000. The original sponsors, as predicted, had stopped giving any money to the club after about three years. There had been no reinvestment in the site, which was a mess, and the academy building was always being broken in to and stuff pinched. When it was moved back to Headingley, Bob Appleyard blamed me for the decision, despite the fact I was not even on the Yorkshire committee, having been voted off in the early 1990s, so I'd had nothing whatsoever to do with the decision. Somehow, perhaps because of my initial opposition, he thought it was my fault.

This old disagreement reared its head when Yorkshire were relegated in 2011. Colin Graves, our chairman, made some very strong comments in the press about the standard of the team's performances, and this prompted Bob to write to him and blame me, for what he perceived to be the lack of talent being produced by the academy. True, I was on the Yorkshire board by this time as the 'cricket' representative, but I had absolutely no power over the academy or anything else for that matter. Stewart Regan, then chief executive, and Martyn Moxon were in charge of that side of things, and (as I was often told by Robin Smith) I merely held an 'honorary position' so could only advise, if ever asked.

In Bob's letter to Colin, he went on to make objections about my personality and even pointed to my court case in France as a reason why I was not suitable to be president. He described as 'the last straw' my letter to Richard Hutton, in which I accused him of living off the family name, an opinion I stand by today. 'The letter is unworthy of a member of the Yorkshire board, let alone that of a future president,' wrote Bob. 'At a time when YCCC needs all the help it can get, I firmly believe we cannot afford conflicts like this … it is clear the last thing we need is for an exodus of members over a Boycott issue, as happened before.'

His attitude seemed to mellow somewhat after I was asked to give a speech on behalf of Yorkshire cricket at a birthday party held to honour Keith Howard, a generous benefactor of the county. He had donated a lot of money so that Headingley could start a museum, which had recently been opened. I spoke about the tradition and history of our great club and mentioned the obvious, more famous past players. However, I could not leave out Bob from that list, and went on to expand on how he was a great Yorkshire cricketer but an unlucky player. In his first season for the county he took 200 first-class wickets, but contracted tuberculosis and did not play again for two years. He came back, bowled fantastically well and was picked for Len Hutton's tour to Australia in 1954–55. If TB had not depleted his health and shortened his career, he might have been one of the all-time great bowlers. He bowled fast off-cutters from a high action. People think of Derek Underwood and how great he was on uncovered pitches, but Bob bowled with the same pace from a higher trajectory and was lethal.

Rachael, among others, said it was as good a speech as they had ever heard me make. Just as we were leaving, Robin Smith told Rachael that after my speech Bob had remarked to him: 'I think we have got ourselves a new president.' Thereafter, the letters stopped. During my presidency he would come to international games, hosted by me in the Hawke room, and attended many county games also in my presence. I know he can be a cantankerous old so-and-so, and I am not saying we are now bosom buddies, but he was always polite to Rachael and me.

I'm delighted to say that, in the end, they were both proved wrong and their predictions never materialised. There was no 'new dark age' or exodus of members and I spent two very happy years as president. In my first season, we won promotion back to Division One in the championship, and then competed for the title in our 150th year, eventually finishing as runner up. Rachael and I organised and ran many successful events to mark Yorkshire's anniversary, raising between us well over £100,000. At the end of it all, I was asked by quite a few members and their committee men if I would consider doing a third year, but unfortunately the club rules do not allow someone to hold the post for more than two years.

A lot of wasted energy in my life has been spent on sorting out problems and issues at Yorkshire cricket. Of course, I know I made mistakes along the way, but I care passionately about the club – I always have done, and always will. Sometimes when I think about all that has gone on over all those years, I am reminded of a quote Margaret Thatcher made. 'If you believe passionately, you will always get opposition – so my life will always be uphill.'

CHAPTER 2

MY GREATEST CRICKETING REGRET

Like most cricket-mad young boys growing up in a mining community near Wakefield in the 1940s and 1950s, I dreamed of one day playing for Yorkshire and captaining the club. Whenever I went to my local nets or matches, Yorkshire cricket would be the only thing talked about. All I ever wanted was to play for Yorkshire. I didn't know if I would be good enough, but I had a dream, a dream that came true in 1962 when I made my debut.

I went on to play for them for the next 24 years until 1986 and captained the side for eight of those years from 1971 to 1978. I am proud to have followed in the footsteps of some great men who captained Yorkshire, but as I look back on my life I realise that taking on the role was the biggest mistake I ever made in my cricketing career. It led to countless arguments with the committee that diverted me from the main job of winning cricket matches, which was made hard enough by the inflated ambitions of other people, who had failed to realise times had changed.

The pressures and demands of captaining Yorkshire persuaded me to put my England career on hold for three years, losing possibly my best years in Test cricket, and I wonder what I would have achieved in international cricket if I had chosen a different course. Yorkshire cricket has been the love of my life and, even though that relationship has hit the rocks many times, I have always answered its call, returning to the Yorkshire board ten years ago and, as we have seen, becoming club president in 2012.

Just as the presidency was an honour I could not turn down, it was the same 40 years earlier when the club offered me the captaincy. It was a fairytale come true for a young kid who spent his childhood looking up to the men who played cricket for their county. They were superstars in our community, held in high esteem and envied by young boys who wanted to emulate their feats. My heroes were men who had been born and bred in the same communities as me.

The world seemed much smaller in those days. Most of us didn't have television and home computers were many years in the future, so the only way you could find out what was going on in the cricket was by reading the morning and afternoon newspapers, and in the 1950s they were printed in London and Manchester. We read the northern editions, which had reporters dedicated to covering Yorkshire cricket and giving it plenty of space and back-page headlines. What happened there would be the big story every day in the summer months, and the northern papers gave it the prominence the national press now reserves for the England team, so it is no surprise I one day wanted to wear the white rose.

I was lucky that I spent my formative years as a county player under the captaincy of Brian Close, studying his methods and learning something new every day. As a youngster I would field at third man, and not just stand there bored to death. I would watch and try to work out why he made certain decisions. Did they work? If so, why? I studied the way he changed the bowling. Why did Fred Trueman bowl only three overs this morning and then suddenly the spinners came on? Why did he keep moving the field placings? I noticed he was always shifting people around. I wasn't the only one to feel that. I remember one day when Dougie Padgett was fielding on the sweep. Closey said to him: 'Dougie, you are never in the right place.' To which he retorted: 'I have made that many new marks on the ground as you have shifted me, it is like noughts and crosses down here.'

I didn't just watch what he did, either. If I didn't understand why he had taken a certain decision, I would seek out Closey at teatime and ask him, not in an aggressive way, but just to quiz him so I could learn. I was a sponge taking it all in, because he was always active, trying to do something to help us win the game. Nothing was allowed to drift because he was so focused on victory. He was very patient with me, explaining why something would or would not work. It gave me a wonderful insight into how his mind clicked and the way he was thinking ahead. It was a perfect apprenticeship in Yorkshire cricket, and was one reason why I wanted to captain the club.

I learnt very early on that winning the County Championship

was the club's obsession, to the point that it was almost expected that we would win the title. This demand for success was understandable because for many years we had been bloody good at winning it. The official County Championship started in 1890 and in 69 years to 1968 (there was no County Championship during the two world wars), Yorkshire had won the title 30 times, way more than any other county.

As soon as I arrived in the Yorkshire first team in 1962, I quickly grasped it was almost an unspoken duty to carry on the traditions of the past. After a day's play when you were getting changed and chatting, the talk would be about how we were going to bowl out the opposition and get more points. It was all about winning.

In those days, every match was played on uncovered pitches, over three days. There were no questions about over-rates so time was your constant enemy, forcing the captain to think of innovative ways to win because you had to somehow ensure four innings were played in three days. Sides picked up a lot of points only if they won matches, with a few points available for a first-innings lead. This meant that while naturally you didn't want to lose, it was worth taking the risk to try to win.

It was only after my first season that official one-day cricket competitions began and we did not take limited-overs games seriously at Yorkshire. The Gillette Cup started in 1963 and was 65 overs per side. Six years later in 1969 the John Player Sunday League was introduced, followed by the Benson & Hedges Cup in 1972. This was not one-day cricket as we know it today, and we were not very good at it. When the John Player League started, Fred Trueman would bowl off a short run-up with two slips, then when someone cross-batted him over midwicket he used to think they were lucky beggars. We did not change our approach as we were still thinking in terms of three-day cricket. We did not have any nous or feel for the one-day game. For a side that played so well in championship cricket, we did not grasp how to play defensive, containing cricket. Given how attacking we were in the three-day game, it seems odd looking back that we couldn't make the switch.

Not for the first or last time in its history, Yorkshire were slow to change with the times. Others had stolen a march on us and were becoming very good at one-day cricket, particularly our big rivals Lancashire. They showed us up by winning the John Player League in 1969, and the following year they won the John Player League and the Gillette Cup. Their success put more pressure on Closey as captain, when the committee men realised the glory that could be associated with winning a one-day trophy. The Yorkshire public were fed up seeing Lancashire win cups, and at the end of the season in 1970 it was clear matters would come to a head. Closey had missed seven John Player League matches that year through injury, so there was little he could have done about our poor performances, but as usual the Yorkshire committee wanted someone to blame, and made him the scapegoat.

Aged 29 I was approaching my best years and wanted a stable environment at Yorkshire, not the uncertainty of playing under a new captain. At that time, Closey's vice-captain was the late Phil Sharpe and I knew there was a good chance of him being promoted to the captaincy because the committee liked posh amateurs. Phil had been to Worksop College, so he had the right schooling and the correct upbringing, but I did not rate him as a leader.

He was a nice guy but he was in the amateur mould, and he did not share my view of the game. I got the impression that his idea of county cricket was just to enjoy it. Each evening he would sit at the bar having beef sandwiches, a gin and tonic and if he got into a sing-song later on then all the better. He loved singing, when we played at Lord's or The Oval, along with Don Wilson he would often go to the Black & White Minstrel Show at the Victoria Palace in London. They were huge in those days, and often came into our dressing room to watch the cricket at Lord's and The Oval before heading off to the theatre for their show; Sharpe loved being around them. Well, I was more ambitious than that; I didn't just want to enjoy cricket, I wanted to win and to play for England.

Playing under that sort of person did not appeal to me at all, so before I flew to Australia that winter for the Ashes tour, I went to Closey's house. It was the only time I ever visited him there. The house was called, appropriately enough, High Places and I asked Brian if he was going to resign or retire. I wanted to know because I had to seriously think about my position and where it left me if he did decide to step down.

He gave me an absolute assurance he was not retiring and was loving the job. He was sure that the shoulder injury which had restricted him in 1970 would heal over the winter and he would be fine, so I went to Australia with a clear mind because I felt Yorkshire would be in safe hands with Brian staying in charge. I could go to Australia, concentrate on scoring runs for England and not worry about the politics and upheaval at Headingley. How wrong I was.

On the tour I batted well. I scored three centuries in the first four tour matches, but before the first Test in Brisbane John

Nash, the Yorkshire secretary, phoned me at 8.30pm in the evening and said that Close had resigned and the committee had voted unanimously to invite me to be captain. I was so surprised Closey had resigned, but chuffed to bits I had been offered the captaincy. The English media covering the tour wanted to speak to me so we held a press conference the following day.

It was then they told me Closey had been sacked. I was dumbfounded, totally speechless. I felt embarrassed because I had accepted the job thinking Brian had resigned. Later on I found out what actually happened: I had been elected captain by a majority vote, after it came down to either Don Wilson, the left-arm spinner, or me. The chairman then asked the committee if they could all vote again and make it look good, by nobody voting for Don this time so it would be carried through 'unanimously'. What duplicity and farce! It was a sign of things to come. So it was that my captaincy started with the club being economical with the truth, but that should not surprise anyone, seeing how Yorkshire was run in those days and what would unfold in the future.

While all this was going on, I was busy batting for England and was in the form of my life as we won the Ashes. Going into the final Test, I needed 18 runs to break Wally Hammond's all-time record of runscoring for a tour to Australia, but I broke my arm on a bad pitch at Sydney against Western Australia just before the seventh Test. Graham McKenzie's first ball hit me in the chest from just short of a length, the second ball nearly took my head off and the third ball hit me just above the left wrist in front of my face as I tried to protect myself. I went off to hospital and that was me finished. Even though it was a painful end, it had still been a fantastic tour and I had put Yorkshire to the back of my mind.

In time I returned home full of enthusiasm for the new job and could not wait to get started. I had a naive, boyish belief we were on the verge of great things, but I had failed to grasp two important factors. The first was that the great Yorkshire team of the 1960s had been broken up as players aged and moved on, but new talent had not been nurtured by the club, so the youngsters coming through struggled to live up to the standards we had set in the past. Throughout Yorkshire's history, the committee had not been known for its visionary approach. They just assumed that because Yorkshire had been fantastic in the past, and the county was full of kids wanting to play cricket, everything would be okay. They thought it would continue forever and we had a divine right to be top dog.

However, Closey had been sacked, Ray Illingworth had been forced out in 1968, and Fred Trueman retired in 1969 with keeper Jimmy Binks. Ken Taylor and Bryan Stott had gone as well. So it was that a side that had won seven championships between 1959 and 1968 and two Gillette Cups in 1965 and 1969 was now consigned to history. We were starting a new era, but were ill-equipped to keep up with other counties.

The second factor was overseas players were becoming a real force in the county game, making teams that Yorkshire had beaten in the past a lot tougher to play. All of a sudden when we came up against a team like Worcestershire, who we used to beat comfortably, we faced Glenn Turner, Ron Headley and Vanburn Holder. Nottinghamshire had Garfield Sobers, at the time the best player in the world. Lancashire could pick Clive Lloyd and Farokh Engineer. Warwickshire had Rohan Kanhai in his pomp and Lance Gibbs. Even smaller counties such as Glamorgan had Majid Khan and Gloucestershire Mike Procter. Kent were another exceptional side. They had John Shepherd and Bernard Julien from the West Indies as well as Asif Iqbal from Pakistan. The result was that Lancashire and Kent were dominating one-day cricket. English players were also starting to move counties much more frequently and the game was evolving but we were stuck in a time warp.

By contrast, in order to be able to play for Yorkshire, you had to be born in Yorkshire, which when I was a young kid made it feel as though you were already part of a special club, but now it meant the county was being held back. Talent is vital and once we entered a barren phase our opportunities for rebuilding the side were limited by geographical boundaries put in place many years before. A few players in the past had tried it on and lied about where they were born, but when the club found out they were shown the door, regardless of how good that player was. It was an unbreakable rule. Nowadays it would contravene countless European Union employment laws and a player would take the club to court winning a load of compensation money for discrimination.

Rightly it has now been consigned to history and we have moved on, extending a Yorkshire welcome to players from all over the world, which started when Sachin Tendulkar became our first overseas player in 1992. More than 20 years later, we have had players from almost every nation playing for us and have even been captained by an Australian, Darren Lehmann, in 2002.

But for me as captain in the 1970s, the rules were in place and I had to make the best of it. It was a nightmare trying to convince the ex-players on the cricket committee to think differently. These men had played in Championship-winning teams and could not comprehend change and would not accept that county cricket had moved on. They wanted us to remain a club that was made up of Yorkshiremen but still beat teams boasting players from all over the world. It was an impossible task.

I was lucky I had some fantastic kids in the team. The late David Bairstow, one of my best friends, was never down for more than five seconds. He had such positivity, exuberance and an energy that was uplifting for everybody in the side. I have not known anyone like him in my life. If I had to pick an all-time XI then Alan Knott would be my wicketkeeper, but I would make David twelfth man. In his playing days, his cup was always half full. It was a fantastic trait to be like that and such a tragedy that he later went on to take his own life.

Graham Stevenson, who died earlier this year, aged just 58, was talented but funny as well. Nobody has ever made me laugh as much as he did, he even made the umpires laugh. He also made me swear at him because he was daft as a brush, which in Yorkshire vernacular is said with affection. Setting fields for him sometimes was an art form in itself. He would be late every bloody day, but what a cricketer! The players would not go out for dinner or for a drink without Graham, they never allowed him a quiet night in.

Another key player in my squad was Arnie Sidebottom (father of Ryan), who played 16 games for Manchester United's first team at centre half. He was the best professional I ever played with. If I asked him to turn up at a certain time, he would be there ten minutes early. Ask him to bowl or bat and he would give you everything. He had reddish hair and he would go bright red in the sun on hot days. After one particularly hot day, Graham said to him: 'You look like my red setter.' So his nickname from then on was Red Dog. Phil Carrick, God rest his soul because cancer claimed him far too early, was such an even-natured man.

The good thing about those four kids was that it was a delight to play with them and yet they were also honest. If I came back in, having been given out lbw and questioned the decision, they would say: 'Well, you didn't get right forward.' They were not frightened of me, and they told me the truth. They were lovely guys who gave the side so much.

However, while they were all first-rate county players, we had one or two who weren't quite as good. For example, there was Peter Squires, who played left wing for England at rugby union. He was a brilliant fielder and a wonderful lad to play with, but he wasn't quite as strong a cricketer as the others. You can have great people, but you need to have a lot of talent as well. How do you compete against counties with three great overseas players? It was impossible.

I was also naive about the complexities of the job. The role of captain of Yorkshire was all-encompassing and not just about choosing which bowler to bowl at which end. You had to run the side on the field and organise things off it without any help. It was not like today, when even county sides have a vast array of backroom staff to help the captain. Instead, we had a physio, a scorer and that was it – the captain had to organise everything else.

When Closey was captain on away trips, he was handed a cheque by the secretary to cover our wages. He had to go to the bank when it opened at ten o'clock on the morning of the match and cash the cheque. He was given some brown envelopes with our names on and how much we should be paid, less the tax, and he would fill them with the money from the bank. He would count it out and give it to us before play started and then at 11.30am have to switch on and start thinking about the game. It was amazing the amount of peripheral nonsense he had to do.

During a home Championship match, Yorkshire would have a selection committee meeting for the next few games, with Brian Sellers, the chairman, calling the shots. Sellers would call Closey off the field and summon him into the meeting. While he was in the meeting, whoever was senior pro, for example Fred or Illy, would take over captaincy on the field. When Closey came back on the field, he would tell the senior pro to stay in charge for a few overs until he got the feel of what had been happening.

To make the whole situation worse, he still had no idea of the team that was being picked for the next match. The lads would ask him what had happened and who had been picked, but the committee would just ask Brian his opinion and then dismiss him while they made the decisions. Only at tea time did Mr Nash, the secretary, come in and give us the team news for the next three matches. It was a ridiculous way of doing things, and I would not stand for that as captain. I made myself unpopular with the committee because I told them so.

These people had been all-powerful for years but here was an upstart as a captain, a star for England, who was not prepared to accept the status quo. I thought my argument was reasonable and right, and that I had won them over by saying it can't be right to bring a captain off in the middle of a match when he was trying to win the game. I also pointed out that I was the only county captain not on the cricket and selection committee and spoke out strongly about this. I wanted a say and a vote on the team I was expected to take out on the field. It took time but eventually they agreed. I also told them I was not prepared to hand out the wage packets and suggested the secretary should do that.

Looking back, I can see why I put some backs up, but at that time they did not want to pick a fight with me because when Closey was sacked, the members had risen up in revolt. They had played merry hell with the committee, there had been petitions and groups formed calling for some committee men to resign. It was a little taste of what would happen subsequently when they also sacked me as captain. The members were angry with the committee over Brian's sacking and that winter Sellers, a former captain who was an autocratic leader, stood down as chairman of the cricket and selection committees to appease the members. However, nothing really changed because he stayed on the general committee, where he was able to still rule the club with an iron fist.

The new chairman of the committee was a weak, malleable man in John Temple, a nice guy who was popular and the perfect character to calm the storm. The peace was short lived, as I soon raised another issue with them where Yorkshire seemed to be operating in a very old-fashioned way. When I took over the captaincy, there were no fixed-term contracts for the players, and I'd seen the difficulties this caused for Closey and Illy. So I put it to the committee that we should have proper deals in place, which made me even more unpopular with them.

The situation was this: Yorkshire gave players a yearly agreement, starting on 1 August and running until the end of July the following year. Why it started in the middle of the summer season is anybody's guess. There was absolutely no sense in that arrangement. When a player was first signed up, the club wrote to him and said it would employ him for a year and specified the salary it would pay him. It was also agreed that the committee would let him know by the end of July whether he was being retained for a further year. This meant there was absolutely no security for players, who feared that a drop in form or a bit of bad luck with injuries could cost them their livelihood. To have that hanging over a player in the middle of a season was not a way to get the best out of them.

In those days, of course, cricketers did not earn very much money and there were no agents to find them commercial deals. Even senior players suffered under this system. In 1968, when Ray Illingworth asked for a three-year contract to have a bit of security late in his career, he was refused. Brian Sellers said to him: 'If you want to go, then you can fucking well go. Fuck off.' He actually used those words. So Illy went, joined Leicestershire and won trophies. His life was all the better because he left Yorkshire and earned himself a decent contract.

It was a ridiculous situation, and I knew I had to address this issue because it was causing so much trouble in the dressing room. Tony Nicholson, the fast bowler and another man who died too young, helped me because he was good at buttering up the committee men at the bar. Between us, we also squeezed more money out of them for the players. But it did not do me any good standing up for the team, as the committee resented me for it.

There were some good men among the 23 on the general committee, but most of them were weak. I do not say that with nastiness; they just did not want to challenge the cricket committee, which was mainly made up of ex-players. Many on the general committee would look up to them, as former stars of Yorkshire, and believed that they would know what they were talking about when it came to cricket and what cricketers wanted. After all, they'd been there themselves, so surely their opinions had to carry more weight. Non-cricket people often find it hard to speak out against men who have perhaps been brilliant at cricket in their lifetime. How do you convince people like Brian Sellers, who had been amateur captain of Yorkshire, that he is wrong? Herbert Sutcliffe was another on the cricket committee, he was a great player. And then there was Don Brennan, who had also played for England. These guys were not bad men but they were stuck in their ways, and they did not realise that the game had moved on since their day.

As the team became poorer in ability the harder I tried and the better I batted but it made no difference, we were just not good enough. So when Yorkshire wanted someone to blame, they decided to point the finger at me. I accept we did not play very well. We finished 13th in the Championship in my first year and won just four matches, though incidentally I made runs in all of those wins. I averaged 109.85 that season and I gave the team everything as I tried to lead from the front. Things were no better in the John Player League, where we finished 16th, winning just five games and losing nine. We had not made any progress from Closey's last year.

That is when all the backbiting started. Whenever I went to

a cricket committee meeting there were complaints. The same thing would happen at selection meetings, and it became fashionable to blame me for all the problems. When I left Yorkshire to play for England, my back was turned and there were plenty of trouble-makers willing to slip a knife between my shoulder blades. The more runs I scored, the more the team failed and some people tried to match the two events as if they were linked in some way. Yorkshire had become a one-man team and I was accused of being obsessed with my own scores. The facts speak for themselves, though, and there was no escaping the simple truth that we needed an injection of new blood, but Sellers had been burnt by the sacking of Close and was not about to rock the boat by ripping away years of tradition to sign overseas players.

In 1972 we improved, in one-day cricket at least, peaking in a Benson & Hedges Cup semi-final win over Gloucestershire at Headingley. They had Mike Procter in the team, who was one of the world's star all-rounders at the time. I read the pitch well and realised we needed five seamers, so I put them in to bat. We bowled them out for 131 in 55 overs. I knew the only way they could win was if Procter and Jack Davey, a good left-arm seamer, took early wickets, because it was likely to seam around all day.

So I defended against those two, kept my wicket intact and waited to score off the three other bowlers. While I was winning the match, not looking to play shots but stay in, one or two in the crowd started to shout out. They had no idea of the pitch and thought we should knock off 131 quickly. One guy shouted out in support of me: 'Whatever thou does Geoff, they will sack thee.' How prophetic. I was man of the match, and scored 75 not out as we won by seven wickets. We'd nullified their threats, as Procter took none for 34, Davey bowled nine overs taking one for six.

We were favourites to win the final because of my form, but on 5 July in the first round of the Gillette Cup at Headingley, Bob Willis hit me on the finger, splitting it open, and I had to be rushed to hospital, given an injection and put to sleep so they could operate. It was like a squashed tomato and I missed the Benson & Hedges final. If I had made 30 or 40 runs, we might have won it but Leicestershire, captained by Ray Illingworth, beat us, so then I got the blame for not playing with a load of stitches holding my finger together.

The opposition was in full swing now, with Richard Hutton the chief protagonist. At one point, he tried to organise a letter to be sent to the committee expressing a lack of faith in my ability. The players refused to sign and it fell through. My relationship with Don Wilson was also strained and he seemed obstructive towards much that I tried to do. It felt like I was batting with a sack of coal on my back; the burden got heavier and heavier and weighed me down.

Of course there were things I could have done better; I hold my hands up. I wasn't a good man-manager, I accept that. I was a strong-minded individual, so I tackled the committee about things and answered them back where perhaps I could have been more diplomatic. I took on senior players, so should not have been surprised when the whispering campaign against me began. When that happens it erodes trust and quite honestly my nature would not allow me to give in and admit failure and defeat. The determination to succeed and tenacity that helped me bat in the toughest situations was, in this case, my undoing.

Remaining captain in that atmosphere was such a mistake. The job brought me so much pain and trouble. It wasted so much time and energy, which I could and should have put to better use by pouring it into my batting, I just did not have the brains to pack it in. I should have learnt from history. Herbert Sutcliffe had the foresight to avoid the job and the strain that came with it. In 1927, he was offered the captaincy but turned it down because he knew it was the era of the amateur captain and it would be a burden and distract him from his batting. He was smart; I was not.

The guy who had best of both worlds was Len Hutton. When he became the first professional captain of England and went to Australia in 1954–55, he just had five Test matches to worry about. There was no media intrusion, no interviews about your personal life, no press conferences at the end of each day. Cricket writers wrote about the cricket. There was a manager on tour who handled everything off the field. In England, he would play five Tests as captain, but in between he would go back to Yorkshire, play under amateur captain Norman Yardley and just bat without any pressure. It must have been a lovely respite for him.

He had the status of being England captain but no outside problems of handling a committee and the politics of Yorkshire. Years later, Len spoke about me as captain of Yorkshire and spotted the difference between my era and his. He clocked the media in my day were far more dogged and summed it up in Alan Hill's book on Herbert Sutcliffe entitled *Cricket Maestro*. Hill wrote that Leonard had told him I was a 'prisoner of circumstances'. That was a very interesting and astute judgement.

It made no difference how many runs I made, the team were just not good enough. I loved the challenge of tactics, changing the bowling and field placings, I had the mind for those aspects of the job. Man-management, diplomacy and PR were not my strong suits.

I was not a political animal; I could not toady up to the committee men, pour drinks down their necks at the bar and make them feel important. I was too focused on the cricket. Alcohol and pubs were a big thing in cricket then. Everybody would go to the bar every night, but I didn't. I remember the first time I played for Yorkshire seconds, Brian Sellers came to the match and bought everyone a drink, even the kids would have a beer. When asked, I said: 'I would like an orange juice, please.' He replied: 'If you want an orange juice, you can buy your own bloody drink.' That was the culture. Brian was not a bad man, but he thought if you had a drink it would solve everything. It was a very macho approach.

My Uncle Algy got it right years ago. He used to say: 'Buy them a couple of drinks and they are on your side forever.' I was not made like that, but I was not smart enough to see I was fighting a losing battle.

It was no surprise that the plotting behind my back happened in a pub. They staged their meetings at the Half Moon in Collingham, north of Leeds, which is ironic because now I pass it on my way home from Headingley to my new house in Boston Spa. This was where the committee plotted to get rid of me as captain and stuck knives in my back. They thought it was a secret, but what they didn't know was that Terry Brindle, who was the cricket writer on the *Yorkshire Post* through the 1970s and 1980s, lived in Wetherby four miles away and often went to drink there. They tried to get him in their camp to write bad stuff about me, but he refused.

Among those who met there to try to get me deposed were Don Brennan, a real wannabe who lived in the past; he was a former England wicketkeeper full of strong opinions. Then there was Captain Desmond Bailey from Middlesbrough, who was all port and hot air. Harry McIlvenny, Brian Sellers, Billy Sutcliffe (son of Herbert) were all also involved. Terry Brindle would humour them, so they thought he was on their side but would then tell me what was going on, hence I was far better informed than they thought.

My mind became so frazzled by the end of the 1974 season that I decided the thing to do was give up playing for England and concentrate on Yorkshire. I felt the only way to succeed was to captain and play every match for Yorkshire. Without my runs they were poor and I could not serve two masters at once. I issued a press statement at the time saying I was going to stay in Yorkshire and find out who my true friends were (I did not say and I would also find out who my foes were).

Having recently met Rachael, the other love of my life, the next season was one of the happiest times I spent at Yorkshire as we managed to come second in the Championship, which was a great achievement with the young team I had. That kept my detractors at bay for a while, but it did not last and for three years between 1974 and 1977 I played only county cricket, which was far too long away from the international scene.

During the time I didn't play for England, they were losing Test matches and the Yorkshire committee were telling me that I should be batting for my country. Then, when I decided to make myself available to play for England again in 1977 and

Yorkshire lost a couple of matches in my absence, they criticised me for not being there. What was I supposed to do: cut myself in half and give one bit to Yorkshire, the other to England? That is how stupid the situation had become by the end. It was a no-win situation, but I would not let the captaincy go until they finally sacked me. How foolish was I?

I am sure I would have played with more freedom and scored more runs in the 1970s if I had never captained Yorkshire. Don't get me wrong, I always loved the Yorkshire members and was passionate about playing for the county, but the people who were running the club made it at times unbearable for me. The rulers had a history of doing what they wanted and sacking players seemingly on a whim. The only difference with me was the members were finally sick of their petty jealousies and decided enough was enough and toppled the committee after I was sacked as a player in 1983.

It is ironic that they blamed me for the uprising. 'Boycott caused all the trouble,' they say, as if I could have canvassed all those people personally to take a stand in 1983. Nonsense! The committee were the ones with the power to make the decisions, not me. They started the unrest, they did the sackings and they reaped what they sowed. They were the ones who underestimated the members, and forgot it was a members' cricket club and not a private gentleman's club run for their own gratification. Sadly, in all the years since, not once have I ever heard one of those committee men say they were in the wrong.

CHAPTER 3

MY WORLD COMES
CRASHING DOWN

My nightmare began on Wednesday 14 August 2002 with an everyday event: I was having a shave.

I felt fit and healthy, and only two days previously had been working at Trent Bridge for ESPN television commentating on a Test match between England and India. My television career was going well and, for the first time in my life, I was about to get married, having become engaged to Rachael on her 50th birthday the previous May. But that August evening at the Atlantic Hotel in Jersey it all changed.

I had flown over because one of my best friends, David Falle, had asked me if I would speak on the Wednesday evening at the Royal Jersey Golf Club. I was getting ready for the dinner and had a shave. While stretching the skin on the left side of my neck, I noticed it seemed to feel unusually firm, and something was just not right. I kept poking around but couldn't find anything specific to cause concern. My health was good, I did not feel ill and had no symptoms other than this baffling firmness. I even began to wonder if it had always been like that and I'd somehow never noticed. However, I knew it hadn't been there when I shaved that morning.

I went to the dinner, and when I came back I had another look at my neck: it was still hard. The following morning I did the same thing and whenever I went back to my room that day I would check again, and it was still firm. It was puzzling and a bit worrying, because I knew that if you found a small lump or unusual swelling the advice was always to go straight to the doctor.

After a day and a half of poking around, I went to a doctor in Jersey; he had a look at me, was not happy and told me I needed to see a specialist as soon as I got back to Yorkshire. When I flew home on the Sunday, I decided to put my fears to one side and not tell Rachael or our young daughter Emma about the lump. I didn't want to worry them, especially as the next day we were due to host a special lunch at our house in Woolley for the Indian cricket team.

I had been doing a lot of commentary in India at the time, so I'd got to know the Indian lads well, and some of them had asked me if they could visit my house when they came to England. They had seen pictures of this old farmhouse with lots of greenery, a six-foot waterfall in the garden and all this space, which they do not get much of in the Indian cities. So I said yes, but I was not going to go to a lot of trouble unless it was put in their official Tour itinerary, as I wanted to be sure they would definitely turn up. The lunch was kept very private, and the whole team came, along with coach John Wright, the team manager, physio and even the bus driver. I invited only eight close friends: Richard and Allison Knaggs, Tracy and Alison Jackson, Malcolm Guy, and Janet Bairstow with her two young children, Jonny and Becky, as well as one very special friend, an Indian reporter called Debu Datta.

Thinking our Indian guests would like some familiar food, Rachael had organised the Aagrah Restaurant to come to the house and cook for them (in fact, Sachin Tendulkar said he would just love a steak). It was only when they arrived that she realised, after Emma told her, that the Aagrah chain of restaurants is Pakistani and not Indian. She was slightly embarrassed and joked that they might 'nobble' the Indian team, Pakistan's fiercest rivals, before their match against England. However, she need not have worried as the food was excellent. The chef and all the waiters were more interested in being in Geoffrey Boycott's house and having photographs with me, than seeing or meeting any of the Indian cricket team.

The chance to talk about cricket with the Indian lads helped take my mind off my personal worry. It was a gorgeous sunny day, and Emma and the Bairstow kids organised a putting contest on my golf green – she even lent the young 17-year-old wicketkeeper Pathiv Patel her left-handed putter. My good friends Sourav Ganguly, VVS Laxman and Rahul Dravid wanted to watch films of me batting and insisted Rachael find some old videos and put them on, while I sat down with Sachin, who had asked if he could have a private chat about his batting.

After that we went into my conservatory to talk to the seam bowlers and I told them: 'Look, you can't win this Test match if you go on bowling like you have been [England had scored

487 and 617 in their first innings in the first two Tests]. Wickets are costing you over forty runs per wicket, and let me tell you at Headingley there are no draws – you either win or lose! Get it into your head: be positive about winning. If you bowl like you are, you will not win; you have to bowl a more disciplined line around off stump.'

I asked Sachin how they could win with this bowling. He said: 'Geoffrey, you are right. I had never thought about it like that; we would need nine hundred runs.'

I then went through all the England players and told them where to bowl. I don't know if this chat made a difference, but it helped me at a time when I was very worried about my throat. It was marvellous to see Sachin go on to score 193 and they won the Headingley Test by an innings and 46 runs, having lost the first Test at Lord's and drawn the second one at Trent Bridge. Before anyone accuses me of not being supportive of the England team and of being unpatriotic, they didn't ask me for any help. If any player of any nationality asks me for help, I give it gladly because lots of people gave me free advice and help throughout my career if I approached them.

The next day, I went to my local GP to obtain a referral to see an ear, nose and throat specialist. On my return home I got into a trivial argument with Rachael; she was standing at the kitchen sink at the time and accused me of being very 'tetchy' with her. When she said that, I just blurted out the reason I had been to see the doctor: I had something wrong with the side of my neck and he had referred me to a specialist the next afternoon. Fortunately, Emma was not present at the time and we decided to keep our worries from her until we knew more information, but I was already really concerned.

I still had a very busy diary, and first thing the next day I was due to go to Headingley, as Fred Trueman, Brian Close, Ray Illingworth and I were jointly opening the East Stand. Once again I had to appear normal and smile for the cameras. I didn't speak to anybody about my cancer fears, although it was a relief that I now had Rachael in my confidence.

After the ceremony I went to see the ENT specialist, Ian Fraser, who had very kindly agreed to see me at his home near Harrogate, and he arranged for me to have an ultrasound later that week. In the meantime, I had to put everything to the back of my mind again as we had arranged a dinner that night at our house for my ESPN colleagues Sunil Gavaskar, Ravi Shastri, Harsha Bhogle, Navjot Sidhu (the mad Sikh who I love dearly), and Alan Wilkins, the former Glamorgan player. ESPN boss Huw Bevan was also there, as we chatted and looked ahead to the Test starting the next day on the Thursday. This time Rachael cooked steak and kidney pie and they all loved it.

I mentioned to Huw, nobody else, that I needed to get away on the Friday of the Test match for a 1.30pm medical appointment. I did not go into details or tell him it was for an ultrasound at Roundhay Hospital in Leeds. But at that appointment they told me they had found a small node in my neck, and tried to reassure me by saying it could be one of a number of things. I just sensed that was not good news. However, I could not dwell on it as I needed to immediately return back to commentating on the Test match.

I thought I had kept it a secret, but the next day when I got home from commentating at Headingley there was a message on my answering machine from Fred Trueman, who worked for the *Sunday People* newspaper, asking me what was wrong with my throat as he'd heard there was a story coming out the next day.

A colleague in the media then telephoned that evening and asked if there was any truth in me having cancer because it was going to be in the Sunday papers. Apparently someone had recognised me at Roundhay Hospital, asked a member of staff what was I doing there and they had been told I had throat cancer! I was very angry. Some sections of the press really are unbelievable. The news was out there that I definitely had cancer; not that I maybe had cancer or that I was just having tests. No, according to the papers Geoffrey Boycott had cancer. In their rush to get a 'scoop' they did not even think to ask me; they did not give it a thought that maybe no actual diagnosis had been made by the doctors and I had been told it could be harmless or a benign lump.

Our daughter had gone to stay at her grandma's in Whitby, so Rachael had to ring her mum and Emma to explain that a story was going to appear in the papers the next day but that it may not be true, and I was just having tests so hopefully would be fine. Emma was only 13 at the time and we should have been allowed to protect her, and to have told her in our own way. Thank goodness Fred thought to warn us of the pending story and she did not have to see it first in the Sunday papers. It would have been a horrible way for her to learn about my possible illness. I phoned Fred later to thank him for tipping me off. Rachael then spent the rest of the night ringing other family members and close friends, explaining that it still might be nothing at all and the reason we had not said anything was there didn't seem any point in worrying people unnecessarily.

Next day all hell broke loose, there were press men everywhere when I arrived at Headingley for the fourth day of the Test. The secretary of Yorkshire said there were journalists and photographers asking for extra passes to the game, but he had refused most of them and told them to pay at the gate. I declined all approaches but could not stop them taking pictures of me. When I phoned the lady in charge at the hospital, Pat Oldfield, to complain and ask her to find out who had leaked the story, she was very apologetic and did later come back to say they couldn't find the culprit.

While I felt my diagnosis was not looking good at that stage, I had not been told I had cancer and there was still hope, yet here it was, all over the bloody national daily newspapers, telling me and the whole world I had throat cancer. I still don't know exactly how the press got hold of the story, but I suppose people do a lot of things for money or perhaps it was just loose talk.

My next appointment was for an x-ray on my chest on Wednesday 28 August at the Bupa Methley Hospital, which was clear, and provided a small piece of good news. I then went into the Bupa Roundhay Hospital two days later and stayed in overnight because they wanted to take out the lump and have it biopsied. It later turned out, when I went to see the oncologist she would have preferred them not to operate, as she was concerned that when they removed the lump any cancer cells left behind may have entered my blood stream – not exactly the kind of news you want to hear.

But it was too late, the operation had been performed and I just had to wait for the results. I tried to keep our minds off it all by taking Rachael to Old Trafford to watch Manchester United play Middlesbrough along with my best friend Richard

Knaggs on Tuesday 3 September. It was an evening match and we were having dinner before the game when the ENT specialist phoned my mobile and said: 'Look you had better come and see me tomorrow morning.' We knew then for sure it was not good.

Next morning my GP's nurse, Julie Huxley, took out the stitches on my neck from the operation and I then went to see Ian Fraser at the hospital at 12.30. He said they had found cancerous tissue in the biopsy. The news left me numb; it was the worst moment of all, because everyone knows that so many people die from cancer. I had known it was coming, but I still went very quiet. My mind started racing: What do I do now? What happens next?

When I got home, I phoned Huw Bevan and explained the diagnosis and said that I couldn't commentate at The Oval Test the following week. I knew that from then on I had to concentrate on the cancer and work out how the hell I was going to stay alive.

Initially I was consumed by fear, facing life and death decisions. Over the next few weeks I would experience the emotions of anger, confusion and desperation as I faced the greatest battle of my life. I was nearly 62 years old and had never smoked or been a drinker. I had never drunk spirits or even a pint of beer in my life, just the occasional glass of cinzano bianco with lots of lemonade or maybe a glass of champagne or wine, so I couldn't understand the diagnosis. Like everybody else faced with such a situation I was asking: Why me?

Without any discussions with Rachael, I not only cancelled my flights to Australia for the upcoming Ashes series but also my credit cards, memberships and annual subscriptions because I thought there was no point in looking to the future when I knew I could be dead.

It was Emma's 14th birthday on 5 September, so she came home that night from her grandma's house as we had previously organised a party for her the next day. She was also due to go back to her boarding school, after the long summer break, three days later on the Sunday. We had to explain to her that I did have cancer after all, and there were tears all round. It still breaks my heart just thinking about that moment. Having to tell this to my only child, especially at such a young age, is probably one of the hardest things I have ever had to do. It was all very distressing, and made me cry. I felt I had been given a death sentence.

Nowadays I am not ashamed to admit it, but at the time I was embarrassed, ashamed and upset because over the next days I would often go into a room on my own and break down in tears. A grown man crying, it was embarrassing and I would try to hide it, even from Rachael. It was so distressing, my mind was in turmoil and I could not think straight, my head was in a total spin. I was getting angry at myself because here I was breaking down all the time.

After a few days of this I had to tell myself: 'Listen, crying ain't going to make you better. If you just sit in a corner and keep crying you sure as hell are definitely going to die.' So I said to myself: 'What are you going to do about it? Pick yourself up and give it your best shot. Whatever it takes, be positive. This is ridiculous: I have always had patience, concentration and been mentally strong with my batting.'

On the Friday afternoon, Rachael and I saw Mr Fraser again and he accompanied us to meet Jamie Woodhead, the local cancer specialist at Cookridge Hospital in Leeds. Mr Woodhead said the tumour was about the size of an old six-pence coin, and he believed it was a secondary tumour and that the primary needed to be found which, if Rachael remembers correctly, he said could come from only one of three places: either behind the nose, in the palette or in the tongue.

I had all weekend to think about this and try to get used to the idea and on the Monday we returned for me to have an MRI and CT scan. Afterwards we met with Brendan Carey, the specialist who had read my results, and he said that I was lucky. (I did not know it then but 'lucky' was a word I was to hear a few times over the next months.) He told me I had two further secondary tumours in my shoulder and one in the neck but they had not spread to my body.

I asked why that was lucky, and he replied: 'If it spreads down in to your body, you have only a five per cent chance of survival.' I was stunned.

He also told me something quite revealing. He said the scans had shown that I have a baby spleen, which was about a quarter of the normal size, and he was quite puzzled by it. It was a shock to me as well. I explained that when I was eight, I'd had my spleen removed after rupturing it when falling off the railings in my back garden and landing on the upturned handle of an old mangle. During the night after the accident, while asleep, I had been bleeding internally and my life was saved only because my grandmother came to the house very early the next morning to see how I was. Recognising something was wrong she insisted the doctor be sent for and I was rushed off to hospital to have an emergency operation to remove it.

Your spleen stores the antibodies that fight off infections and that is why I always had problems. In the 1960s and 1970s I was wary of going to play cricket in India, where conditions were harsh and infection a real danger. As Brendan Carey explained, the surgeon must have left behind a very small bit of my spleen after the operation and over the years it had grown, so I did have some, if not a lot, of protection after all.

It was not the only shock of the day. In the afternoon Rachael and I went to the Bupa Roundhay Hospital to see Mr Woodhead again who now, having studied my MRI test results, told me I had a tumour the size of a small orange at the base of my tongue.

Having been told I had a tumour about two centimetres wide, suddenly now I have one six centimetres wide; this was a big change. He said he needed to operate quickly and had a slot for surgery later that week. I remember sitting there thinking that a small orange seemed bloody big and feeling taken aback that it was in my tongue and not my neck. I'd had no symptoms, could not feel anything unusual on my tongue and had no idea how this had happened.

I was in a fog trying to get my head around it all and suddenly he wanted to operate immediately. In my confused state, I worried that if they could get the size of the tumour wrong once, they could get anything wrong. So I told him I needed to go home and have a bit of time to think about what I wanted to do. When I got back home I began searching round to get help and information, as it was a hell of a big call I was having to make.

I phoned Professor Ken McLennan on Saturday 14 September for some background information on tumours and what to do. Meanwhile, around this time, we were fortunate enough to start receiving books and magazines through the post from well-meaning people who had read in the newspapers about my cancer. I could not focus on them, but Rachael felt she needed to look at everything. Some books were from America and full of medical jargon, and they were not clear about what was best to actually do and she just flipped through those.

The one book that immediately stood out was called *Everything You Need to Know to Help You Beat Cancer*, written by Chris Woollams. It was a simple paperback, very easy to read and understand for anyone without medical knowledge or training. Most cancer books tell you what not to do; this was the opposite and told you what you should do. When she gave it to me, I couldn't concentrate long enough to fully understand what I was reading; I was dealing with too many emotions so Rachael went through the book again and highlighted the parts which she insisted I should read and from then on it became our bible. I spoke to Chris on the phone and he has been there for me ever since. Even now we occasionally have a catch-up.

The first thing he said when I got in touch was: 'Let's try to work out the cause.' He asked if I smoked or drank or used mouthwash, to which the answer to all three was no. So he then said the only thing he could think of was that I must have picked up a parasite while travelling somewhere like Sri Lanka, India, Pakistan or Bangladesh. Apparently a parasite can produce toxins and carcinogens that can cause inflammation in the gut, which in turn has an effect all around the body. He told me to take a course of ParaFree to kill any parasite and also to balance my gut bacteria with probiotics, as I could not get better until the bacteria were killed off. He then went on to tell me about milk thistle and a liver flush using Epsom salts and how I should take daily exercise.

Chris had only recently started to dedicate his life to researching cancer therapies and cures. His teenage daughter Catherine had been diagnosed with an incurable brain tumour and told the medical profession could do nothing for her. Not wanting to accept this, he used his skills and knowledge from his MA in biochemistry and set off all over the world researching a cure for her.

Miraculously, he managed to get her into remission for a time but unfortunately it returned in later years and sadly his daughter passed away. On the back of her initial recovery, Chris formed a charity, CANCERactive, and a monthly magazine called *Icon*. Chris's work and charity have gone from strength to strength since then, and he tells it very straight. He is not afraid of the big drug companies, who make fortunes out of producing cancer drugs, and he says many people are dying of ignorance not cancer. His philosophy is to arm you with as much information as possible, so that you are better able to make your own choices, because each person's cancer is different. He does not advocate alternative therapy, and his advice is designed to complement treatment from your oncologist, not replace it. I can honestly say Chris helped us more than any other person, and Rachael is convinced if she had not been able to keep falling back on his advice, I would be dead. I have to agree with her.

Chris has a 15-point checklist of what people should do when they discover they have cancer, and number one is to find a 'cancer buddy', someone close to you who can help take you to appointments, listen to the doctor's comments and advice (as you never take it all in), check your medicine and offer support during the dark times that inevitably follow once the treatment has started. He warned me that the punishing nature of chemotherapy and radiotherapy would leave me lifeless.

He said I would need a 'buddy' to help me get up in the mornings, cook my food and also try to ensure we lived a vestige of a normal life, my mind would be frazzled with the pain and discomfort and I would need a rock. For me that meant Rachael, I was lucky. Chris also emphasised the importance of home comforts in helping me to fight the disease. This turned out to be vital advice for me, because a few very well-meaning people had recommended different hospitals and doctors in places as varied as New York, Switzerland and London. But being treated at one of those hospitals would have required weeks renting an apartment or staying in a hotel having room service and being away from my family, friends and home life.

It would also have separated us from Emma, who was away at school in the week but came home most weekends. Her presence would be hugely uplifting and important to me during my months of treatment and she often helped her mother, not least of all by ganging up on me when I needed bullying! Living in a hotel and a strange environment would have added more stress to Rachael, who had so much on her plate already, and in those circumstances you do not want any additional worries.

Caring for someone with cancer, or any serious illness, is a tremendous burden and immensely stressful. I have nothing but admiration for people who dedicate their lives to looking after a loved one, sacrificing so much for the care of someone else. If that patient dies, they can often feel a sense of responsibility as if they failed in some way. Coping with the grief of loss is hard enough, but to think you failed a loved one in their hour of need must be unbearable, even if other people tell you that there was nothing more you could have done.

Rachael admits she knew from the beginning it was not going to be easy and felt quite emotional at the enormity of the task. She thought it was her responsibility to make sure I lived, not just for her and me, but for Emma's sake too. She believed that if I didn't make it, it would be her fault. So Chris's advice rang true straightaway and helped us decide to stay at home in Woolley.

One of the main things he also told me to do when I rang him was that it was imperative that I detoxed my whole body and change my way of eating. Changing my diet was no problem, but he also wanted me to have a coffee enema, which Rachael bought at the chemist as a DIY kit. She read out the instructions to me, and it was only then that I realised I had to shove it up my arse! She explained that I had to lie on the tiled bathroom floor, because it might make a mess, and that she would do it for me if I was not going to do it myself. I said to her: 'You ain't shoving anything up my arse!' The idea was dropped. It was the only piece of advice Chris gave us that I didn't follow – and I'm bloody glad I didn't.

Rachael had already been contacted by Sarah Surety, a feng shui lady we knew, and she too had mentioned the importance of detoxing and she also knew a nutritionist not too far away, Stacey Darrell, who could help. So I rang Stacey and she travelled from her home in Pickering, North Yorkshire, and stayed with us for three days and two nights to go through everything and show Rachael what foods to cook and what to throw out of the cupboards. She made me eat only miso soup for two days and drink lots of water, but this had to come from a glass bottle as nothing stored in plastic was allowed.

She left her menu book with instructions I could have lots of vegetables cooked a certain way, brown rice with tahini (sesame paste) and eventually I would be allowed white fish or chicken but no red meat or any dairy products. Everything had to be freshly prepared and organic where possible, with no ready meals allowed. Rachael had to get a soya margarine called Pure and use only a natural fruit sugar in my food. She got some oat milk in the end, because soya milk was just too sickly for her, as she had joined in eating the same things I did, in order to support me.

A friend of mine suggested I start taking a tablet called Revenol (an antioxidant) and put me in touch with Caroline Carey, who was an agent for a company called Neways which sells complementary therapies and treatments. Caroline suggested I also chew some apricot kernels, which contain the natural compound amygdalin (or B17), as they are believed to aid cancer treatment.

I asked Chris Woollams for his take on this and he confirmed the Revenol helped stop inflammation, among other things, and he explained how to take the apricot kernels. Apparently they can be helpful to some people, but he warned that I should never chew more than five or six in any 90-minute period, with a maximum of about 35 a day. I had to be careful because they contain cyanide, and people with cancer also have liver problems so I would need watching. If I turned a bit yellow or grey then I had to stop taking them. He also advised me to increase my intake gradually each day, starting with only five a day.

Later on, when my cancer treatments were decided by the oncologist, Chris drove up to see me. He built a programme of supplements for me – antioxidants mainly – that I should start taking before and after the chemotherapy. When it was time for my radiation, I had different tablets before and after as recommended by him. Among others he suggested fish oils and curcumin, which is derived from turmeric, to stop inflammation. I liked his honesty about what to do and was grateful because he did not try to fool me with empty promises. Nobody can give you guarantees when facing cancer.

Over the weekend of 14 September friends who had survived cancer were in touch offering advice. Paul Sykes, who built the Meadowhall shopping centre in Sheffield, came to see me and told me he went to the Johns Hopkins Hospital in Baltimore in the USA, for prostate cancer treatment. Because of the superb experience he had there, he donated millions of pounds for a new cancer wing at St James's University Hospital in Leeds, which was being built to replace the old ramshackle Cookridge Hospital I attended.

Another friend of mine, Russell Homer from Jersey, said he could put me in touch with John Watkinson at Queen Elizabeth Hospital in Birmingham, who is a specialist in cancer of the thyroid and he would be happy to give me advice and help, so I spoke to him. He was very positive and confident. He asked if I minded him making some enquiries on my behalf at the Cookridge Hospital. I was like a sponge soaking all this up, I wanted as much information as possible. When John got back in touch, he said he had learnt the operation would take eight hours. He said the surgeon would have to break my jaw in order for him to be able to remove the tumour, then my jaw would be re-wired shut for it to heal and I would not be able to talk for six weeks. As Rachael kindly pointed out, not talking for six weeks would be a problem for me especially!

He went on to say his information was that Mr Woodhead had been in the job for only a year and, while he was very good, it was doubtful he had done this operation before. Apparently the cancer specialist who had been his predecessor for a lot of years had just recently died himself from a brain tumour.

This information threw me into doubt about whether or not to have the operation. The clincher for me was when I asked John what he would do in my position, he replied he would not have the operation. He said there were only three surgeons in the UK he would want to operate on him to treat this type of cancer. One of them was Professor Pat Bradley, who worked only for the NHS at Nottingham General Hospital and was also the chairman of the British Association of Head and Neck Surgeons. John agreed to phone Pat Bradley on my behalf on the Sunday, and an appointment was set up for a consultation at 2pm on Tuesday 17 September in Nottingham. He would then perform the exploratory operation first thing the next morning. Pat said he wanted to knock me out and have a look down my throat himself, in order to be satisfied exactly where and how big my tumour was.

On Monday 16 September, Rachael and I attended the oncologists' clinic at Cookridge Hospital at 9.30am, meeting my oncologist Catherine Coyle for the first time. Jamie Woodhead, the surgeon, was also there. I told them I had decided to seek a second opinion and was going down to Nottingham the next day to see Pat Bradley.

It's about an hour's journey down to Nottingham from Woolley and Rachael insisted she drive as I couldn't concentrate on anything. Pat's a gregarious Irishman and he made me laugh when I joked with him that he'd better not have any Guinness that night if he was operating on me the following morning. He reassured me he did his best surgery the day after having a few drinks the night before to relax him. Rachael and I went to stay in a hotel that night, as we had to arrive back very early next morning for my operation as Pat was doing me a big favour by fitting me into his busy schedule, but neither of us really got any sleep.

That morning, I went down to theatre and Pat took nine biopsies and had a good look around. He then came to see me in my hospital bed a couple of hours later and told me straightaway I had a tumour as big as a 50 pence piece. He also said it was too large and too close to my voice box for him to guarantee, if he operated to remove it, that I would not lose my speech. He explained he would need to take out a larger area than just the tumour to make sure of removing all the cancer cells.

If the worst scenario happened during the operation, then obviously my quality of life would suffer as I would not be able to speak. He said I was lucky because the tumour was on the left side of my tongue and not across the mid-line. Apparently that was important because the blood supply for the tongue is down the middle. If any tumour goes across it, then they have to cut out the tongue because it would never heal and would just be dead meat in the mouth. He said he would operate if I wanted him to, but his recommendation was I have chemotherapy and radiation treatment instead of surgery. He added that, because I had not smoked or been a regular drinker of alcohol in my life, my chances of success with chemotherapy and radiations were nearly as good as having surgery.

He warned me that the tumour was now so big I would need to decide quickly. He also mentioned that once they operated they could not then go back to chemotherapy and laser treatments; I had to choose either one or the other. I asked him what would happen if I did nothing. He replied: 'I give you three months.' In other words, I would be dead just after Christmas.

I can tell you that being given three months to live is a real showstopper. I remember he also looked Rachael straight in the eye and said: 'You will be surprised how many wives of very successful men can't cope with their partner's cancer and are not still with them at the end of it all; Geoffrey will need your help.'

I did not really grasp what he was saying, but Rachael knew immediately that he was warning her it was not going to be easy, that it was going to be tough on her too, not just me. Pat said he knew my oncologist in Leeds and would send her his report and I must then decide what I was going to do. When Rachael eventually drove me home, we travelled pretty much in silence as we were both a bit numb at what we had heard and at the enormity of the decision we were facing.

Out of the blue on the next day, a Macmillan nurse, Julie Hoole, called at the house. We were baffled as we did not know she was coming or anything about what Macmillan stood for. They offer you expert help, information, advice and support, free of charge when diagnosed with cancer. I was not really clear what she could do for me, unlike a lot of bread-winners to the household who have to stop work, I was very fortunate that I did not need financial help and felt she was there more as a sympathetic ear for someone who needed a crutch at such a distressing time. I thought it was very kind of her to come, I was not ungrateful, but I could not see what she could give me.

Meanwhile, I had to decide what was the best practical course of action for me. It was a horrific dilemma, as I had no medical training to help me, but in the end only I could make the decision. I opted for the chemotherapy and radiation.

Once I'd made my decision, Catherine Coyle, having received Pat Bradley's report, called me in immediately on the morning of Friday 20 September. It was now that I got to hear from her the problems I would face and how difficult it was going to be for me. Fortunately it turned out to be a case of 'we' and not 'I'. We were working together, and I soon came to realise that there was nobody better in the world to help me fight cancer than this frank and feisty, nearly 40-year-old Irish woman. She was dead straight with me, which I liked about her. Some people may not want to know the truth, but I did. I asked her if the treatment was going to be tough.

'Yes, very,' she said.

'What? Really tough?'

'Really, really tough!'

'Jesus Christ!' I replied. 'What are my chances?'

She answered that they were about 80 per cent. 'Can you give me ninety per cent?' I bargained. She was firm, and didn't try to be over-optimistic; she stressed that my chances were really good, and in an entirely different bracket from what they would have been if I had been a smoker or drinker. I then said: 'Well, if you save me I will kiss your arse' to which she blushed a little and laughed.

Catherine then asked me if I was on any tablets, so I explained about Chris Woollams and told her I was taking complementary stuff. Like most of the medical profession at the time, she did not really believe taking these types of tablets or going on specific diets helped with cancer, but she was open-minded enough to realise it was my body and I was going to do it regardless. All she asked was that I gave her a list of what I was taking at any given time, which I always did. In the weeks that followed there was only one herbal tablet she asked me not to take and explained why she thought it might interfere with what she was prescribing.

She wanted to give me two separate sessions of chemotherapy, the first starting that very day, so I was admitted into Cookridge Hospital for what was to be five days and nights of treatment. It started in Room 20 of the Rutherford Ward – I can still remember it now. I had a machine pumping horrible chemotherapy drugs, 5fu cisplatin it was called, hooked up to a vein in my arm 24 hours a day. It was not pleasant; Rachael likened it to mustard gas. What it does is kill all the fast-growing cells in your body, but unfortunately it does not discriminate between good cells and the cancer ones.

It was not immediate but eventually the drug destroyed all my saliva glands, and to this day they have unfortunately never come back. The chemotherapy also destroyed my taste buds, which did regenerate after about 12 months, and all my immune system, which took the best part of two years to be re-established.

While I was in hospital having this treatment, they also took me down to the 'Mould Room', as they called it, where they measured me up for the plastic mask I would need to wear during radiotherapy.

When I was discharged on 25 September, Catherine told me I had to see their dentist the next day to check all my teeth. It was the first I had heard about this and I wondered why I needed to go – I had cancer not cavities. I had been told I could be dead in three months, and so I was desperate for them to get on with the treatment, yet here they were sending me to the dentist.

Unbeknown to anybody else, 26 September was the date Rachael and I had made an appointment to visit the Register Office in Wakefield, in order to post the banns for our marriage. When I got home and told Rachael I had a dental appointment the next day, she just stared at me, and then I was reminded what we were supposed to be doing. There was so much going on I had forgotten all about it, and I said 'Oh fuck! I will cancel the dentist.' She said that we could reschedule the Register Office. In fact, when I rang to say we would have to cancel the appointment and gave them the reason why, the lady at the Register Office said she would come see us the next day at Woolley.

I wanted to get married before the treatment took hold, because if I died I did not want the tax man to get all my money, as I feel I have paid enough of that in my life. Rachael joked she was not too proud about the circumstances behind getting the ring, as long as it finally happened after all the years we had been together.

At the dental clinic I was told there was a problem with a

couple of my teeth, one in particular, a big molar on the right side. It turned out there was a gap between the tooth and the gum, and if it got infected with any bacteria it could be a serious problem once I started the radiation treatment. Osteoradionecrosis, as it is called, is a complication caused by radiation, because it impairs the blood supply to the bone in your gums and it dies. I was told removing my teeth would delay the radiotherapy for two to three weeks, because they would have to wait for the wounds to heal fully before commencing treatment.

I was angry. My teeth seemed healthy to me and I did not want any of them taken out. I thought that with cancer, time was of the essence, yet this had been going on since late August and here we were almost in October and I felt I still had not started the real treatment. I had only had some chemotherapy, but no laser treatment. They seemed to be taking forever and now they wanted to add in more delays while they took out some healthy teeth. I had cancer in my shoulder, neck and tongue, but I felt that if we had carried on like this I would end up having the most fantastic set of teeth in the morgue.

This was when I had a stroke of luck. As I had just come out of hospital after my first round of chemotherapy, the discharge liaison nurse from my GP's practice, Julie Maltman, came to see me early that evening, completely unannounced. She turned out to be a star. I did not know it at the time but our guardian angel had just walked into our lives.

I chatted to her about my teeth and she arranged for me to see another dentist in Heckmondwicke, Naresh Sharma, and he passed me on to his friend, Professor Monty Singh Duggal, who is head of child dental health in Leeds. He was brilliant and solved the problem. He confirmed there was one tooth which was a candidate for infection, as it did have a small gap where the gum had receded, so he gave me a syringe with corsodyl, an antiseptic and disinfectant, and told me to inject the hole every morning and evening. In fact I am still doing it today, 12 years later. The tooth has never been taken out and must be the healthiest, cleanest tooth in Yorkshire.

My life now consisted of an endless round of appointments. I had a 'mask fitting' on Tuesday 8 October at Cookridge, which took around three hours, it's not exactly like being fitted for a new suit. The next day saw me back again as they needed to look at my kidneys to check for damage caused by the chemotherapy, and that took approximately four hours, so along with the two-hour round trip in the car, another day was gone.

On the Thursday, we had arranged for a Chinese feng shui master to come up from London, with his delightful personal assistant, Jan Hassan, to visit our house in Woolley. I was open to anything, just trying to find things to help me stay alive. Rachael had dabbled in feng shui for a few years, so she persuaded me to have someone come and do a more personal reading for myself and our house. Rachael knew there are bad and good health 'houses', and felt we needed to have our home checked out.

My close friend at the time, Russell Homer, had used this particular feng shui master for his home in Jersey, so on his recommendation I got in touch with Master Li. We had previously furnished him with the exact time and dates of birth for Rachael, Emma and myself in order that he could prepare our individual readings before he came. He did not have a clue who I was, and in his broken English kept referring to me as

Mr Geoff because in his culture the first name is considered to be the polite way to address someone. His assistant Jan also had no idea about cricket or who I was or what I did.

Master Li explained that there is a health area in every house and we should have a small light on 24 hours a day in that area. He also advised us to put a water feature in the kitchen and he told me in what direction I had to sleep, with the back of my head facing south/south east for the rest of that Chinese year. Apparently you heal as you sleep, so it is important to know where to sleep. Rachael therefore moved me into a small single bedroom to accommodate this and also the chair in my 'snug' was moved in to a 'good' direction. He added that our health moves in ten-year cycles and mine had started when I was seven years old; he said it was written in my chart that I was going to have health problems from ages 57 to 67. Looking back that had been the case, but this was the most serious health problem by far.

He also said I would need to celebrate my 70th birthday with a big party, which we eventually did, but at the time I was not sure I would make that milestone. However, Rachael says that is when she knew, without doubt, I was going to survive this, and that is what kept her going in the 'terrible times'. Deep down she always had this certainty in her mind I would live.

On Monday 14 October, I made another journey to Cookridge for Catherine Coyle's review clinic and I weighed 85.4 kilos fully clothed. She told me to eat as much as I could because I would need to keep my strength up over the coming days, and she advised me to take regular exercise, so after my treatments in the morning I would go for a walk in the afternoon in Woolley Park.

The following day I returned for another mask fitting and then on Wednesday I had to attend a round of blood tests for the chemo treatment. Catherine Coyle told me she had booked me in for Monday 21 October to start my second round of chemo. I asked if I could go in the day after, as it was my birthday and I wanted to celebrate my 62nd because I thought it might be my last one. I did not tell her the real reason was that Rachael and I had scheduled our wedding for that day.

Catherine didn't want to delay things even by one day, however, as her tests had shown the first set of chemotherapy had been too strong and had destroyed too many white blood cells. Apparently there is no 'set dose' for this treatment, and the dosage is usually calculated on the basis of one's weight. She had originally wanted to give me five more days of chemotherapy, but could now give me only three days and she said this made it even more urgent to start the radiation treatment. So after the chemo gave my cancer its first powerful kick, I started laser treatment on Tuesday 22 October while still in hospital. It was the first of 35 daily sessions that ran for five days a week for seven very long weeks.

She explained that the effects would be particularly grim, because she wanted to give me the most aggressive dosage she thought I could stand, at strength 70, rather than the 50 or 60 which is more usual in the UK. Apparently she had done her training in France where this is the norm. Looking back I am glad I had her and that she was confident enough in her own skill to do this. It was bloody painful but I have no doubt it was one of the things that saved my life. Pat Bradley later said I was lucky to have her.

CHAPTER 4

THE FIGHTBACK BEGINS

At last I felt I was really beginning to move forward. We are constantly bombarded with advice telling us the importance of how catching cancer early can make the difference between life and death, but from the date of finding my tumour shaving in the mirror to having my first zap of radiation had taken almost ten weeks. Even if you take it from the date when it was confirmed as cancer, which was the night I went to the football at Old Trafford, then it had still taken seven weeks for the treatment to start. During that time I got increasingly angry and frustrated, because I wrongly felt it had been strung out for so long. I did not grasp that, by having the chemotherapy sessions, I had in fact already started my treatment. What was more, because of my name, I had been lucky that so many people had come into my life and helped speed things along.

It is during this period that cancer patients can become

irrational and feel life is unfair. The fear of dying grips your every waking hour, and yet the medical profession appears to be taking forever to start the treatment. While you want to rip out the tumour which is slowly snuffing out your life, they seem to be stalling. I now know that this is unfair, because the doctors have to pinpoint your treatment in order to make sure they do the right thing for you. But that was how I had felt in the few days leading up to my radiotherapy finally starting. Perhaps I would not have been so desperate to start had I known the pain that was in store for me.

During my chemotherapy treatment Chris Woollams had suggested I take something to counteract the side effects and to stop me vomiting. Thankfully it worked. He also warned me before I started my laser treatment that I needed to understand chemotherapy kills and destroys all the fast-growing cells in the body, and if my body was left to its own devices it could take up to two years for it to be fully restored. The immune system is so weakened by the treatment that you are vulnerable to viruses and illnesses during that period and for a long time afterwards.

With having only a small spleen I was even more susceptible to infections than normal, so had to take special precautions. Chris taught me the trick of putting Vaseline in my nostrils when I woke up in the morning. The hairs in your nose are the first line of defence for any airborne diseases and need to be moist and sticky to trap any germs. I did this whenever I went to hospital, as that is where the risk was at its greatest. A number of times I arrived at Cookridge and would see people there for treatment, and friends or family who had brought them to the hospital, sniffling. I was starting treatment just as we were heading in to winter, a season when colds are commonplace, so the risk was high. Even the receptionist was coughing and sneezing a lot one day, and I remember her saying she thought she had flu. If I had got anything it would have been very difficult to shake it off. The Vaseline must have really helped as I never once caught a cold, and I still keep up this treatment even now when travelling on a plane or any place where the air is circulating around. As a result, I've not had a cold to this day.

Chris sent me a tailor-made list of the herbal supplements he wanted me to take, as well as details of when to stop some and then start others. So I began taking different tablets to assist my body, and particularly my kidneys, to flush out all the dead cancer cells that he said would now be floating around my body after the chemotherapy.

In fact all around me I was receiving great support, and on the Friday after coming out of hospital, I rang my then boss at talkSPORT, Kelvin MacKenzie, to give him an update. He was fantastic. I know he can be over the top and divides opinion, but I loved working for him and knew I would have a job to go back to if my health returned, which took that particular worry out of my life.

For the next seven weeks our daily routine had to revolve around the trip to Cookridge and back. I had set my mind to recovery. This was what I needed to do: I counted the 35 sessions off like I would my runs when I was batting. I always had a gift when I was batting for knowing my own score. I counted every single one of them in each game I played and I did not need the scoreboard to know what I was on. When I played in matches with a primitive scoreboard or not very reliable scorers,

I would know if they had my score wrong. In one-day cricket I used to count my runs, how many an over we needed to win and whether we were above or below the asking rate. I went about it in exactly the same way when I had my treatment. I would count each and every one until we got to the halfway mark. I then felt I was heading for the finish line. I would fall asleep thinking: 'I have done five; it will be six tomorrow.' I focused on that to get me through.

My appointments at the start were at 9am, which was the first of the day, but in order to not be late I would have to set off by 7am. It was only about 20 miles away, but it necessitated going up the M1 and then through the centre of Leeds to get to the hospital, which was in the northern suburbs, so it wasn't straightforward. As time went on Rachael said this is silly and the radiologist agreed to move my session to just before lunch, which was more convenient in some ways, but more often than not I would have to wait a long time for my turn.

One day I went for my treatment and there was a young boy aged eight or nine with no hair left and he wouldn't or couldn't take any more. His mum, the nursing sister and head radiologist were all trying to persuade him to go in for another session of treatment, but he just sat on the chair in the waiting room with his head down, not talking. He'd just had enough. It was heartbreaking to see this small, scared child in such a state, but the shocking thing is it is a scene played out in every hospital, every day. As I looked on, the nursing sister, Sally Marshall, said to me: 'Don't miss any sessions, Geoffrey.' She then explained how my treatment had been worked out in advance and if I missed one they would have to recalculate everything. I said I wouldn't and I didn't.

I would have laser treatments Monday to Friday, with what Catherine Coyle called a session review every five days. The actual laser bit of the procedure would take only two or three minutes each time, but getting ready for it was another ball game. I would go into the treatment room and they would put my plastic mask in place. It looked so grotesque; I resembled the man in the iron mask. There were two holes for my eyes, two small ones for each nostril and a slit for my mouth so I could breathe. I would lie on the table and the mask would be bolted down with screws on either side of it.

In order for the technicians to know exactly where to blast my neck, Catherine had previously marked the mask with a cross where she wanted the laser to be aimed. It was imperative my head stayed absolutely still, because if the rays hit my spinal column I could have been paralysed from the neck down. Meanwhile, the laser would move on its own accord as programmed, to various angles starting on the good side of my face, the right side, before moving to the left where the tumour was.

In the early days of this treatment, I drove myself to the hospital and could not see any marks on my neck. I was eating normally, if you could say my new food 'regime' was normal, and taking a daily walk in the park. It didn't seem as bad as I had been led to expect. By the time I had my first session review after five days, I was starting to get a dry mouth, even though I was producing more mucus than normal as a side effect of the chemotherapy.

It was on one of my weekend breaks from chemotherapy, Sunday 10 November, that Rachael drove me to Leicestershire to see Dr Patrick Kingsley, a specialist in holistic medicine that Chris Woollams had suggested I go see. Patrick asked me to fill in a questionnaire about my life and health, which helped him form answers to the question that had been bothering me from day one, namely: why did I get this cancer? From the answers I gave him, he came up with five possible reasons: dairy intolerance, zinc from my fillings, radiation exposure from flying, inoculations and stress.

It was the first time I had been told I had an intolerance to dairy products. He deduced this from the fact that whenever I had contracted a cold it would always move to my chest and I would then need antibiotics to clear it up. But the most telling factor for him was that throughout my teens I had lots of problems with catarrh and sore throats, leading to my tonsils being removed at the age of 22. This is a relatively late age for that kind of operation and coincidentally my daughter Emma had to have hers removed around the same age, too.

In terms of the fillings, he said that each time I brushed my teeth, in my case two or three times a day, a bit of zinc would go down my throat from my metal fillings. He believed the amount of air travel during my cricket and commentary career put me at risk of accumulated exposure to the radiation we are subjected to on airplanes. People do not realise how much radiation there is in the cabin of an aeroplane. During my life I'd been administered lots of inoculations, in the belief I did not have a spleen and thus lacked natural defences to infections. Research has shown there was a possible link between cancer and hepatitis injections.

Stress was the final suggestion he had. He knew who I was and what I did and pointed out that I had spent all my life as a professional sportsman in a 'goldfish bowl' in front of the media and public. He thought the final straw might have been going through the 'French farce', as the press dubbed it, which was my court case. This came on top of Chris Woollams's theory I had been carrying parasites picked up during my time in the subcontinent, which is why he had previously recommended I take the ParaFree drug and probiotics. Finally, I was starting to find some clarity as to why I had contracted this horrible disease, but now the most important thing was to concentrate on the cure.

Before we left, he took lots of blood samples to send away and said I would need copious amounts of vitamins and supplements to combat what my body was going through. He recommended intravenous injections as being the quickest way to do this and suggested I get in touch with Dr Damian Downing, a nutritionist based in York. This was something we had never heard of before, but now once a week Rachael would drop me off, giving her time to escape and do the food shopping, while I would have a drip put in my arm and instantly fall asleep for an hour. I have since learnt that nowadays celebrities are apparently having these intravenous sessions before their gigs or heavy nights partying. For me the reason was very different.

On 14 November, Catherine Coyle made an appointment for me at the hospital with Hayley, her nutritionist, who explained that they would need to fit a tube to feed me when the pain from the burns in my mouth and throat became too much to bear. I was strongly against this suggestion and looking back I think I saw it as a sign of weakness and was determined to stay away from it as long as I could, even though eating food was beginning to become more difficult.

We tried to keep life at home as normal as possible, and

Rachael insisted from very early on that no one was going to die and there would be no pussyfooting around me in the house by anyone. She decided for all our sakes that it was important, when we could, to keep some humour and laughter in our lives. She used to say to me when I was being un-cooperative or grumpy: 'Stop it! You are just ill, you are not dying!'

I remember that on the weekend of 16 November we took Emma to see the newly released Harry Potter film at the local cinema, because she and I both loved the films and it was important that our daughter had as much normality in her life as possible. It was fortunate that she was at boarding school and not there all the time, so Emma did not see me distressed and in difficulty every day.

By week four the pain had started to increase and the burns on my skin really hurt; it was agony. My brother Tony or the local taxi driver, Mick Hough, had been taking me to my daily appointments for some time, but now I needed Rachael's help. As the radiation built up, I developed terrible raw burns and they had to be covered up in case of infection. First to go was the skin on my collar bones, then my neck and eventually the skin on my left cheek. We were given some pale pink sponge-like pads that needed taping over the open wounds. When it was removed, if any of the tape even touched what looked like good skin, it would rip it off and cause agony.

Rachael devised various shapes in order to fit the afflicted areas and eventually I had pads all round my neck, which she said made me look as if I was wearing a vicar's dog collar. Before the radiation started they would take the burn pads off and that was the worst moment of all; the pain as the cold air hit the burns was enough to make me want to scream. It would last only for a few seconds, until they put a protective cling film over the oozing wounds, so the pus did not get on the mask during treatment, but of course the pain would start over again when they removed everything.

While I was having my sessions every day, Rachael would find a vacant nurses' room nearby and get some fresh burn pads ready, she would usher me in and cover up the skin as hastily as possible. The nurses would not always be free immediately I came out of the treatment room, as they were often busy with other patients, so they did not mind Rachael doing it instead, as it ensured I did not have to lie there in agony waiting.

Although the skin was now badly burnt, every session made it worse but I had to keep going for more treatment on red raw skin. It needed all my mental strength to get up in the morning, go to the hospital and have more radiation. Every brain cell is screaming at you not to go, but you have to fight the temptation to give up and stay at home.

I was still travelling to York for my vitamin treatments, even though by now I needed Rachael's help just to get me dressed in the mornings. Unfortunately, I was no longer getting any effect from my pain-relief tablets, so eating was becoming tough. Rachael had been mashing up all my food into a puree, so it was like eating baby food, and she had even been crushing my tablets into powder and putting that in the food so I could swallow them. But because the pain relief was not working anymore, I was finding it increasingly difficult to swallow anything.

Our guardian angel, nurse Julie Maltman, came to the rescue. She brought me some morphine pain patches to put on my arm, which slowly infused into my body and helped stop the pain. When I first started using them, I began with one patch at strength 25 and it lasted for 72 hours. However, the more treatment I had, the worse the pain; I had to increase the number of patches, so I ended up with three, the maximum dosage allowed.

As my treatment continued, my energy levels started to deplete so I spent most of my time at home just lying in my reclining chair. I was so tired and weak when I came back from the hospital I did not even want to get up and go to the toilet. I would watch television in the afternoons, something I had never done in my life, but as I was quite doped up I would fall asleep, so I might see the beginning of a programme, but very rarely stayed awake to the end.

Ironically, I found that my favourite programme was *Ready Steady Cook*, in which two contestants, one wearing a red tomato apron and the other a green pepper, competed against each other, with the studio audience voting as to who had cooked the better dish. It was weird because I could no longer eat, had no appetite or even any taste buds left and I had never been interested or watched anything remotely like this. Rachael would have to watch it wherever she was in the house, because if I missed the ending I had to know who had won.

Despite how I was feeling, every morning when I got up I would force myself to go for a walk because at that time I would be at my freshest. No matter how cold it was, I would still go out, wrapped up in an enormous overcoat and scarf. By this time I had stopped walking into the village, as Rachael was concerned I might collapse. I worked out if I walked 20 laps around our tennis court it was close enough to a mile and she would keep checking I was okay from the house, while she was doing the chores.

By Wednesday 4 December I was losing weight alarmingly, and had shed ten pounds in one week. Rachael had shopped to buy me some trousers that did not fall off me and also bought some thick woollen cardigans, as I had no proper winter clothes. It was the first whole winter I had spent in England for nearly 40 years, and I hate the cold. The burn blisters in my mouth were agonising; we have thousands of nerve endings in our gums and on our tongue, and I had huge blisters every-where in my mouth. They were raging sores that even the slightest touch would aggravate, so eating food was impossible. It was a tough time and I was getting seriously ill.

I was now sleeping all the time because of the morphine, not eating and even struggling to drink. In fact water was the hard-est thing to swallow, even more than pureed food. It was obvious I could not go on much longer like this, but I still had four of my 35 sessions of radiation treatments to go. It is not just what the cancer does to you, it is the treatment. I kept resisting having the feeding tube inserted, because I somehow thought it would indicate I had given up and the disease had defeated me.

I had been going to my weekly review sessions and trying to fool them when they weighed me by stuffing my cardigan pockets with heavy coins and putting a handkerchief on top to stop them clinking together and alerting them to what I really weighed. I knew that once I fell to a certain weight, they would insist on putting what I thought was this horrible tube up my nose, so I did my best to delay it as long as I could. I feared it because it was the unknown and also the kind of thing worn by really sick people. Of course I was sick, but I did not want to admit I had fallen to such a low ebb.

Looking back now, I realise my subterfuge was only making matters worse. In the end they saw through it and, as Rachael says, I looked so god-awful anyway. After weighing me that day, Sally Marshall went off to speak to Catherine Coyle, who came straight away and said: 'I want you in hospital now!'

I tried to bluff her and said I would need to go home to get some clothes, but she was having none of it. My weight was dangerously low and I was having the tube fitted there and then whether I liked it or not. There are two options when you are having a tube fitted: either you can have one straight into your stomach through an opening, but Chris Woollams had advised me against that due to the possibility of infection, so I opted for the tube through my nose. This involved a nurse inserting it up my nose and telling me to swallow so it could be pushed down in to my stomach. It was not a very pleasant experience but actually, like most things in life, the fear and dread of it happening was actually worse than the event itself. I had to just accept the fact I was now going to be fed by a machine.

It was hardly an inconspicuous piece of kit, and I was not going to be able to hide it from public view. For a start the tube was yellow, not skin-coloured, and taped to my nose where it came out, to keep it secure. It went across my cheek, rested on top and behind my ear then dangled down to my chest. On the end of the tube was a tap or port, as it was called, and through this my medicines and water would be inserted with a syringe. When it came to feeding me, each time a new sterile tube would need fixing to the port, which then ran to a bag of liquid feed and that was hooked up to a machine that pumped it into me. I needed two and a half bags a day, which would take about eight hours.

The following day when Rachael returned to hospital, the nurses showed her how to use the feeding tube. They said I would not be able to go home until they were satisfied she knew how to deal with it. The first step was to make sure it was still going down into my stomach. They explained that at no time should I ever be allowed to lie completely flat, even through the night, in case I coughed it up into my lungs, which could have lethal consequences should liquid then be poured down it. Using a syringe attached to the port, Rachael would draw some liquid and test it for its pH value on a piece of litmus paper. The tube would then need rinsing out with a clean syringe full of sterile water, before the feeding process could begin.

A few weeks previously, knowing the tube was inevitable at some stage, Rachael had asked the dieticians at Cookridge what was in the bags of feed they would be giving me. When they told her it was lots of goodness mostly consisting of milk and sugar she had pointed out that I was intolerant to dairy and that cancer loves sugar. The nutritionist said there was no alternative, but fortunately Rachael had her wits about her and knew there was a soya feed that Chris Woollams had told her about. Hayley had never heard of it and was sceptical but promised she would look into it. About three days later, she phoned Rachael saying she had tracked down the soya feed and ordered a case of 12 bottles for a start and would keep it ready for me when I needed it. She was a lovely lady and so helpful.

In time we became accustomed to using the machine and found when at home the best way to encourage the fastest flow would be for me to lie in my reclining armchair in the snug with the pump propped up high on an antique plant stand. It was quite a sight, and apart from anything else Rachael would joke that my nose, all squished up with tape holding the tube in place, made me look like Michael Jackson. I did not care; I was relieved because it meant an end to the constant fear of eating or drinking and the dread of having the tube fitted was over.

Unfortunately, at the same time the tube was fitted the hospital staff were given orders to take me off the morphine patches because they were too expensive. It was a bitter blow, as it meant I had to take the medicine through the tube and, unlike before, there were now periods when I had to wait for it to kick in.

On my third day in hospital, Rachael had to learn how to administer the liquid morphine down the tube, and what a palaver it was. She had to check the tube was in my stomach, wash it out, put the red medicine in, wash it out again and then hook it up to a feeding bag. They even wanted me to learn how to do it as well, but there was no chance I could manage it. The new drug routine had started on 4 December, when I was given two millilitres of pure morphine to control the pain every six hours, and if the pain got worse I could have an extra 20 millilitres of a diluted morphine if I requested it. It seemed a fairly straightforward system.

As I only had one session of radiation left, on Monday 9 December, they decided I might as well stay in hospital over the weekend so the nurses could keep an eye on me. However, I had already made plans for the Saturday night and the Sunday morning, so it was agreed I could be 'sprung' out of hospital for these, as long as I returned.

Months before I knew I had cancer, I had booked for the three of us to go to the Grand Theatre in Leeds to see *The Nutcracker*. I enjoy the classical ballets and Emma, like most young teenage girls, loved dancing and she had never seen a live ballet performance. Rachael went home on the Friday night leaving me with strict instructions to be dressed when she arrived back with Emma the next afternoon, before we went out that evening. She was concerned that Emma, not having seen me for a couple of weeks, would be distressed enough at my appearance dressed, never mind how I looked undressed. By now, having lost 50 pounds (about 22 kilos), I resembled a wizened old man of 90, while naked I looked like I had just come out of a concentration camp.

When they arrived in the ward, Rachael was met by the nursing sister who explained that unfortunately that afternoon I had gone to sleep flat on my bed and had coughed the tube out. Apparently, I had agreed to wait for her coming to discuss if it should be put back in before we went to the ballet. Rachael was not best pleased after all the instructions she'd had the day before about ensuring she did not let me lie flat, but suggested it would probably be best to leave the tube out until I returned from the theatre. She knew I could still be recognised in the audience when we went out, and it would be kinder not to have people staring at me with a yellow tube across my face.

I cannot remember them walking into my room, and I am told it was not a pretty sight with me lying on the bed naked and then jumping up in an agitated state trying to get dressed. Rachael says Emma was obviously taken aback, but then just hugged me and helped me to dress.

I really do not recall much at all, but I liked the show and

Emma tells me I was grinning like a Cheshire cat at people. I tried to drink some water from a straw during the interval but struggled with that. When we left the theatre and went back to the car, Emma says I walked straight into a lamp-post with my shoulder and bounced off it and said: 'Sorry, I apologise.' Emma whispered to her mum: 'Dad is talking to the lamp-post.'

Rachael got the impression that if she had said 'jump off that cliff', I would have said 'yes, dear'. As she said later, this would have been most un-Geoffrey like! When we arrived back at the hospital, Rachael parked right outside the entrance to my wing and put me in the lift, which I had been in many times before. I needed to get out at the second floor, and as the corridor had all-glass windows, they could watch from the car to make sure I walked into the ward. I had to turn left into my ward, while the main hospital, which was pretty much in darkness with it being a Saturday night, was to my right. What did I do? I turned right and disappeared out of their sight. Emma then rushed up the stairs to find me and take me back to my ward and handed me over to the nurses.

The following morning Rachael was at home with Emma fast asleep in our bed, when the phone rang next to it. As she remembers it, she heard my croaky voice at the other end say: 'What time is it?'

'It's eight thirty.'

'In the morning or at night?'

'In the morning. Why didn't you ask the nurses?'

'Why? Where am I?' I replied.

'You're in hospital, love. In Cookridge.'

'Thank fuck for that. I thought the IRA had got me.'

All I remember of our conversation was waking up in a panic, lying in bed gripped with fear in a sparse, enclosed room with a very small window. I had a tube up my nose and there was a machine on the bedside table. It was dark in there and I was scared to get up. I was staring at the door frightened of what was behind it. I waited for a little while not knowing what to do, then I saw my mobile phone and knowing my home number off by heart managed to ring Rachael.

Because of my behaviour the night before and now this, she knew immediately something was not right and took action. She had to drop Emma back at boarding school that morning for a school trip, so rang Mick Hough, who had been driving me around in the early days of my treatment, and asked him to go and pick me up immediately. She told him not to take any nonsense or arguments from the nurses, and to get me to sign any forms I needed to discharge myself. I was not to walk down the stairs, but to use the lift and he was to keep hold of me at all times. She said he was to bring everything with me, because the duvet, pillows and towels were mine, and he was to tell the nurses I was not coming back. Rachael was not messing around. He did exactly as she had said, and the nurses gave Mick my pain medication, in two separate bottles, to bring home with me.

Weeks before, I had arranged a meeting with my local councillor, Norman Hazell, for that day, so Rachael was due to come and get me from hospital anyway. When Mick got me home, he stayed until the councillor came to drive us to Fitzwilliam, the village where I grew up.

For months I had been lobbying the local authorities to do something to help Fitzwilliam, which had fallen into dereliction since the closure of the mine in the late 1980s. My brother

Tony, a lovely man who helped me no end during my cancer treatment, still lived in the area and his terraced house was two streets from where we grew up with my parents, at 45 Milton Terrace. Tony had been coming to help tend my garden at Woolley and for some time had been telling us horror stories about youths setting fire to the roofs of the empty houses next door to him, stealing lead, downpipes, guttering and using unoccupied houses as drug dens.

He had taken me back to Milton Terrace to see how it had become, and it was a mess. The house we had lived in as kids had been demolished, and was now just a pile of rubble and bricks. The rows of houses still standing were in an awful state, and in my brother's street there were about eight houses, including his, that were still in a good condition and nicely kept, but the rest had either broken or boarded-up windows. If you had seen someone in a 4×4 car, wearing dark glasses with a big AK47 poking out the window, you would have thought you were in Beirut. It was heartbreaking to see the area I loved as a child end up in this state.

Tony had bought his house with his redundancy money when Kinsley Drift mine closed in 1986, but now he was stuck with it. He could not sell up and move away because nobody wanted to buy houses in that area. It was the same for his neighbours; these decent people were living in an awful area and they had no escape route. It was disgraceful and I had pushed for months to organise this meeting at my brother's house with Norman, Peter Loosemore, the Wakefield Council minister in charge of housing regeneration, and Kevin Dodd, the chief housing officer for that area.

The only day they could make was that Sunday so I had to

go regardless of the state I was in. I must have looked almost as run down as the houses, with a feeding tube in my nose, very gaunt and hunched over, but I was determined to make sure these men would take action. After a short chat, I took them round the estate and explained that we needed the council to compulsorily purchase, for a reasonable amount, the houses of the people who were stuck there. The council had already done this for other streets and then knocked the houses down, but Marlene, Tony's wife, had been told it could be a few more years before it would be their turn.

At the end of the tour, I invited the three men to return the following Sunday. I said to them: 'I would like you to bring your wives and I'm going to ask them one question: "Would you like to live here with your children?" One simple question, because I know what the answer will be. If the answer is "no", then why should you expect other citizens to live here?'

I left them to think on that while I went home. Some months later, I was delighted when the council came through for Tony and Marlene with an offer they could accept, and with my help they bought a lovely bungalow nearer to their daughter.

By the time I returned to Woolley, Rachael was back at home and I was due my morphine before she hooked me up to my feeding machine. After a while, she could sense something was not right again; I was hyperactive and could not keep still, so she rang Julie Maltman for advice and, although it was a Sunday, she came straight over. She was puzzled and could not work out why I was behaving so strangely and left saying she would be back the next day. But about ten minutes later, on her way home, she rang from her car and asked Rachael to say what was on the labels of the two bottles of morphine.

Rachael read out the contents and the dosage on each bottle. A light went on in Julie's head: she realised the hospital had mixed up the two dosages. Instead of giving me 2 millilitres of pure morphine and 20 of diluted morphine, they had been doing it the other way around. For four days I had been getting 20 millilitres of pure morphine every four-to-six hours and tripping on one of the most powerful drugs known to man. It all started to make sense: grinning through the ballet, talking to the lamp-post, getting lost in the hospital and fearing I had been kidnapped by the IRA. I had been hallucinating on a morphine high. Julie said I was lucky, for if my system had not already been accustomed to the drug, taking 20 millilitres of pure morphine could have killed me. She told Rachael to flush me out with as much water as possible and to stop the liquid morphine.

When I went to the hospital the following day for my last laser treatment, the nursing sister asked me why I had left hospital the previous day. Rachael relayed the whole story and the cock-up with the medicines. I saw Catherine Coyle two days later at her weekly clinic and while reading my notes she just glanced up at Rachael and said: 'Oh I see you are back on the pain patches, well that's fine.' They both looked at each other and nothing more was said. We could have taken it further with the hospital, but I was alive, thanks to Rachael's intuition and Julie's knowledge.

I was told after the laser treatment finished that the radiation would still be in my body for two to three weeks, a bit like a microwave I would still be 'cooking', and as it turned out I was in real difficulty for the rest of December.

When Emma came home for her leave-out weekends, she was always full of energy and her mum made sure she too was looked after. She was a teenager and needed attention from her mum, but Rachael had taught her how to flush the tube and change my feeding bottle to keep her involved in my recovery. Rachael could not leave me on my own, because I was unable to work the feeding machine if anything went wrong, so when Emma came home for the Christmas holiday it was a huge help to her mum and having my 'little nurse' around cheered me also. We had to have as much normality as possible in the house, and Emma taking over the feeding just became another part of our routine.

During this period, Rachael never tiptoed around me, she would tell me off if I was un-cooperative or grumpy, and she became my companion and carer instead of my lover. Her role had completely changed. When visitors came to see me, I would say: 'Have you met my new jailer?' Even though I was now a lot sicker, it was still important to have jokes and laughter in the house to keep everyone's spirits up. Rachael would joke I had saved a fortune having a chemical peel on my cheeks, free of charge by the NHS.

We had a range of people who came to see me, or who kept in touch by phone. Martin Edwards, the president of Manchester United, popped in for coffee one day, while Sally Anne Hodson would often call with messages from her brother Tony Greig. Lots of cricketing friends like Darren Gough, Arnie Sidebottom and Barry Wood either stopped by or called. In fact, Barry relieved me of some of my best red wine on a few occasions. Every other Sunday morning throughout my illness, Fred Trueman rang when he got home from church and would ask Rachael how I was doing. Sometimes I was well enough to talk and if not she would give him an update.

I can remember one time during that period when he was beside himself. He kept saying: 'Have you seen what that pillock Roy Hattersley has written in the Sunday paper? He's been asked to pick his all-time greatest Yorkshire side and he's left you out. Can you believe it? And he's picked two left-arm spinners [Wilfred Rhodes and Hedley Verity] – just shows how much he knows about cricket.'

On Christmas Day, I sat at the table in our conservatory for lunch with Rachael, Emma, Rachael's parents, her brother Mick and his wife Glenda. For their sake I tried to eat some mashed-up food, but really could not manage it. I was in such a mess because my burns were at their fiercest and I had ulcers on the side of my tongue which had grown to the size of the nail on your little finger. My tongue was swollen and grotesque, and if I caught the ulcers on my teeth the pain was excruciating. I had to go back and lie in my chair. When Rachael came in from Christmas lunch, she could tell I was in a bad way. I had a handkerchief coming out of my closed mouth, covering my tongue trying to stop it from catching on my teeth.

Seeing that, she asked: 'You do not have to say anything, but is that to protect your tongue touching your teeth?' All I could do was nod. By this time I had three 25-strength morphine patches on my arm, but the pain was still getting through. Rachael had never sent for my GP, Dr Tony Sweeney, before but I was so distressed she called him and he came out on Christmas Day, took one look and administered a morphine injection straightaway. Alan Knott had phoned me from Cyprus on Christmas Eve and I'd managed a quick chat with him, but when Ali Bacher and Asif Iqbal among others telephoned the next day, Rachael had to tell them I was not well enough to talk.

Over Christmas and New Year the office of Dr Downing, the man I went to for vitamin injections, was closed but a doctor I had met a few years before, David Fieldhouse, came to help. He drove all the way from his house near the Dales to my home on 28 December just to give me this vitamin infusion. I was touched by his kindness.

Chris Woollams had said I needed to have acupuncture as soon as my laser treatment was over, because it would help my immune system get up and running, which in turn would help my energy levels. So I started going to see a specialist in Chesterfield called Robin Crowley who is a master at acupuncture. It meant that I was now having two long car trips every week: one to see Robin and another for my vitamin infusion.

The feeding tube remained long after the radiation therapy finished while my mouth and tongue healed, and it became normal to take the pump with me everywhere. Because it took eight hours for the food to be dripped into my stomach, and you are not allowed to feed while asleep at night, I could not afford to lose half the day not feeding when being driven to York or Chesterfield. Fortunately, the pump could run off a battery so Rachael would sit it on the middle console between the two of us, I would recline my seat as far back as possible to help gravity ease the flow of liquid down the tube. The pump became my constant companion – I even had to take it to the toilet with me. Every week I would also go to Catherine Coyle's clinic, and on Monday 13 January she took the tube out to see if I could manage to eat without it. I was pleased at this sign of progress, but it proved to be a false dawn.

There were other signs that I was getting better. My neck was healing, the dressings had gone and I was starting to look healthier and was down to having only one morphine patch on my arm. I was even able to get out of the house a bit more, and on 17 January I attended a function at the Town Hall in Leeds. I continued to try other therapies that might help. I went to a place in Upton, West Yorkshire, to try reiki, a Japanese therapy which believes in the power of hand healing on the body, but it did not do it for me, and I preferred to stick with the acupuncture.

My television employers, ESPN, had stayed in constant touch and were a great support throughout the whole thing, passing on the many letters and faxes of goodwill they had received from the public in India. They were one of the best companies I have ever worked for. As soon as I had been diagnosed with cancer, I had ceased working but they honoured my contract all the way through my illness. Every month I expected them to stop, but they never mentioned it and just continued to pay a not inconsiderable sum of money into my bank account. I shall always be very grateful for their support and as soon as I was feeling a bit better, Rachael encouraged me to get in touch with them and I did a live interview on the telephone on Tuesday 21 January. It was my first step back into what resembled work.

Three days later, I went to Fitzwilliam to open a nursing home for the elderly but that day I overdid it a bit, spending a long time on my feet, talking to people. When Julie called that night for her routine visit, she suggested I increase the morphine patches back to two because I was in a lot of pain. I was trying to move on with my life and rediscover some normality, but the pain in my throat would come flooding back, reminding me not to get carried away.

Saturday 1 February was the start of the Chinese New Year and in 2003 it was the year of the goat. The previous year I had slept with the back of my head facing south-east, but in the year of the goat I now had to have it facing north-east. The best direction every year is different for each individual, and is still something I practise today. Moving bedrooms felt like a new start, as if we were leaving the bad year behind, but even though we were trying to be normal by going out a bit, I was still not very strong. I remained little more than skin and bone, having lost all that weight and gaining energy was a slow process.

With the feeding tube gone, I was struggling to eat and because I had lost all my saliva glands and taste buds it became doubly difficult to get any food down. Rachael was spending ages in the kitchen, cooking fresh organic food for me, which she would then blend or mash up, to make it softer and easier to swallow. Despite doing all that, she was then still having to cajole or force me to get it down.

Unsurprisingly, sometimes she would get mad and frustrated with me, and I would get very cross at her because she did not seem to realise how difficult or painful it was. She said she was being cruel to be kind; I said she was just being cruel and that was her nature. I did not really mean it, of course; I was just feeling terrible and knew she was fighting hard to do her best for me. She also kept on giving me brown rice, which Stacey Darrell had recommended, but I hated the stuff. I warned her that when I was better, if she ever served up brown rice again she could shove it up where the monkey keeps his nuts! It may be good for you, but I vowed that as soon as I was well, every packet of the horrible stuff would go in the bin.

Eventually, on 12 February, Catherine decided I would need the feeding tube inserted again because for four weeks and three days I had not progressed. Cancer recovery is not a straight line, it has bends and ups and downs. My throat was getting better, then it would get worse, the pain would subside and I would start to get back to normality only for it to return again. It tested my mental strength to accept every setback. I tried to get off the morphine so my body would not become dependent on the drug, but it was difficult as the pain had not gone away. Now, although I had the tube back in, I was still supposed to be trying to get used to swallowing and eating food, alongside the liquid feed. I was trying, but as Rachael says I was very trying for her!

On 14 February, Emma thought I should take Mummy and her out for a meal to celebrate Valentine's Day. We went to one of our favourite restaurants, the Three Acres, and it was a lovely evening. There was nothing on the menu I felt I could get down, so they were marvellous and made me scrambled eggs which I did eat, but when I got home I had to put a patch on to dull the pain. I was so desperate to know when things were going to get better I even turned to astrology. I was just searching for anything to give me hope, to know how long it would be before I was back to normal. Fortunately, I had something to take my mind off my cancer.

CHAPTER 5

REMISSION
AND RENEWAL

The previous year we'd had two abortive attempts to arrange a date for our wedding day, but my cancer treatments had overtaken them and so, after the second time, when on my birthday I was called in to start my second chemotherapy session, Rachael had said: 'Right I am not marrying you until you are well.'

I was not exactly 'well' but my treatments had finished, so we decided it was now time and we set the date for 26 February. We had been through so much and just wanted a quiet day with our family and close personal friends. The last thing we wanted was the press finding out and taking pictures, turning it into a media scrum.

The registrar at Wakefield Register Office helped us to keep it all quiet. The banns had already been posted five months previously on 27 September, before the ravages of the disease had taken its toll on me. Norma Stroud had come to the house to discuss arrangements for us to fill in the forms. Instead of us going to see her and risk the chance of being spotted, and someone guessing what we were up to at the register office, Norma suggested we did not provide our full address and leave out the first line, 'Pear Tree Farm', and just put '2 Water Lane, Woolley'. She explained the wedding banns would be displayed on the noticeboard at the register office, and when the press came in they would merely glance at it on their way upstairs to the deaths department to see who had died. Apparently they usually just looked at the addresses and not the names, because the only people they were interested in seeing getting married were prisoners in Wakefield jail. Norma was right and we were lucky that not one press man had clocked it at that time.

I was not well enough to traipse around a load of jewellery shops, and again we did not want to risk anyone recognising me buying a wedding ring, so Emma went with her mum to choose one. However, I still wanted a say, so told Emma she had my vote as well as her own, because she is very like me and I trusted her to pick something I would approve of. This meant she had two votes so could over-rule her mum, which tickled her pink.

We invited only about two dozen guests, telling them not to be late arriving at our house and to get all dressed up for a lunch to celebrate my recovery. The word 'wedding' was not mentioned in the invitation, but one or two of the females had guessed. Unfortunately my brother Tony and his wife Marlene had already booked to go on holiday so they could not be there.

Everyone arrived at 11.30 and they were then requested to drive down to the register office in Wakefield. Richard Knaggs, my best man, and Emma, the only bridesmaid, knew our secret. The registrar, Mr Hodgson, and his staff were brilliant and kept it all confidential. I was lucky that the press did not have a clue, and the news only came out a few days later, when the marriage had been registered at Somerset House in London.

The news of our wedding was all over the dailies but they had no real details or any pictures, so we had reporters camped at the bottom of our drive for a few days, but to no avail. Then my youngest brother, Peter, started opening his mouth. Again. Although I had no proof, I was pretty sure he had taken money from newspapers during my playing career for information about me, usually when they wanted to get at me for something, and as a result I had blocked him out of my life.

Even when my daughter Emma was born in 1988, Peter had been the only member of my family to speak to the press. Although, true to form, what he told them was a load of drivel, because we'd had no contact for years. When I was starting to recover from the cancer treatment, Tony, our middle brother, who still saw Peter, told me: 'Our Pete would like to come to Woolley and see you.' My first thought was no but Rachael had been working on me, and although I hadn't said anything to anyone I was coming round to it. So, a few days after our wedding, I was really annoyed to see Peter spouting that 'the family knew nothing about it' and 'I wasn't invited and my brother Tony didn't go'. It was as if he was privy to my life, and I was really angry. Unsurprisingly, after that the reconciliation never took place.

For the wedding ceremony, I surprised Rachael and pulled my feeding tube out, but I knew I would need to go back to the hospital the following day to have it put back in. Catherine Coyle was concerned when I turned up without it, but forgave me when I told her the reason why I had taken it out. She congratulated us both and said if the next month went well I would be strong enough to fly long haul if we wanted to go on holiday.

At the time, the World Cup was on in South Africa and ESPN had asked me if I would like to do a little work for them. All I had to do was watch the matches on the television and then they would call me afterwards for a quick interview. It gave me something to concentrate on, other than being unwell and trying to recover.

The other thing that people forget is that, just because you have got cancer, your other illnesses or problems do not disappear. On Thursday 20 March I went to Leeds Nuffield Hospital for an injection in the facet joint of my back. I had first injured it in 1968, playing for England in a Test match against Australia at Edgbaston, and it nearly finished my career. As a result of all this sitting and lying down over the previous few weeks, it was playing up and giving me some discomfort.

Four days later, I was back at Cookridge Hospital to see Catherine Coyle and, nearly 16 weeks after it had first been inserted, she said the tube could finally be removed. For a couple of weeks, I had been slowly reintroducing semi-solid food alongside the feeding tube, but this felt like a significant step in my recovery. Having all of my taste buds destroyed was both good and bad news. Rachael would prepare food I used to like the taste of, with a sauce or gravy to help me swallow, reasoning that if I knew I liked it in the past, it might be easier to eat it. However, unbeknown to me, in order to help me gain weight, she would add loads of natural fruit sugar to my portion and not just in desserts but savoury food, too.

As I started to eat more normally again, I was once more fighting with Rachael over my eating. I would move the food around on my plate, chop it up and play with it or have a nibble, even though there was nothing to chew. Rachael would watch me for a while and then eventually lose patience and say: 'For God's sake, put it in your mouth and swallow. You're acting like a young anorexic girl.' It was as though I had lost the art of eating, I was just not used to it and had to relearn how to deal with food.

Julie Maltman was a great support to both of us. Right from the beginning, she had got into a routine of calling on her way home most nights, having finished work for the day. Julie would have a drink with Rachael and catch up, while at the same time she would be studying me. She would sit at the table with us and try to distract me into eating my dinner. The best at that, though, was Emma. When she was at home she would make me laugh and spoon feed me saying: 'Now that's the way to do it, Daddy.' She thought it was hilarious that even carrots and chicken tasted of sugar and I did not know, but her mother had sworn her to secrecy.

Although I was not gaining much weight, and always had the cancer shadowing my every move, I was thankfully now emerging back into real life. The first step was our family holiday to South Africa, which had been a target motivating me through some of the dark moments of the previous weeks.

On 27 March my two girls and I flew to Johannesburg and then had a car drive us to Pecanwood Golf Estate, near the

Hartbeespoort Dam where my friend Ricky Roberts, who caddied for Ernie Els, lent us his house. We stayed there for a lovely week and I even began hitting golf balls again on the range, but I did not have the strength to play a proper round, even with the use of a buggy. There was a private plunge pool at the front of his home, overlooking the lake and all three of us would go in to relax in the evening.

One night, without my knowledge, Rachael took a photograph of me from behind, towelling down naked. For the second and third week of our vacation, we had arranged to meet up at the Sun City resort, about an hour's drive away, with Richard Knaggs, his wife Allison and my two young godchildren, Richard Jnr and Tara. Once there, Rachael got the photograph printed and gave it to me over dinner. It was a huge shock. She had done it deliberately to show me what I looked like. I was that thin I resembled one of those skeletons you see in the doctor's office, but with some skin still hanging off it. Rachael said she was sick of me 'pussyfooting around' with my food and wanted to jolt me into realising I had to eat properly.

The mouth blisters were all healed but eating normally was still tricky. My taste buds and saliva glands had been destroyed by the treatment and my appetite was a long way from returning to normal. I was managing small mouthfuls but could not cope with big meals. I do not like using this analogy, but to be blunt I looked like someone who had just come out of a concentration camp. I was a shrivelled old man and seeing that picture was a turning point for me. I decided my next goal was to do something about putting the weight back on. I kept that photograph in my wallet for quite a long time and would look at it if ever I needed encouragement to eat.

It was on this holiday that we also started making plans for the future, even though I didn't know at this stage if I had a future. I had always talked about having a house in South Africa, having fallen in love with the country on my first England tour in 1964. A close friend of mine, a Leeds lad actually, had been the golf professional at Stellenbosch in the Western Cape for a lot of years and he had told me about a new Jack Nicklaus-designed golf course being built near Paarl, with plots for houses on it.

Graham Webster rang me to say the developers were releasing the third phase of housing plots that day, so I had the plans couriered over to me at the Palace hotel. Rachael picked the plot that she liked, overlooking the 14th, 15th, 16th and 17th holes, but time was of the essence if we were to bag it. We told Graham which one we liked and he agreed to go and take pictures of the plot straight away. Unfortunately, the weather was wet and misty so when he emailed them to us at the hotel all we could see was what looked like a potato field, but he said it was a superb site and so I bought the plot, unseen. It was something I would definitely not have done a few years before.

Here I was, fighting cancer, still not knowing if I was going to live or die, spending around £140,000 on a bit of land, next to a newly seeded golf course in the middle of nowhere, in a foreign country. Perhaps it made me more gung-ho, but I thought building a house in the sunshine would be therapeutic and a beautiful retreat in years to come. I have never regretted it, and we spend as many English winter months there as my cricket commentary work allows, and I love it.

When we returned from Sun City, the first thing I needed to do was go and see Catherine Coyle for my monthly check-up, and I handed back the feeding machine that had kept me alive for all those weeks. It was a momentous feeling as I looked at it and thought: 'I don't need you anymore, thank you very much.' Rachael's photo had done the trick, I was making myself eat and the fights between us had stopped.

Catherine had explained that while I was in remission for now, I would not be given the all-clear for five years. With my type of tongue cancer if it is going to come back, it does so in 80 per cent of cases within the first two years, so I would need a monthly check-up for the first year and then every two months in the second year. If it hadn't come back by then, there was still a 20 per cent chance, meaning my check-ups would be every three months in year three, every four months in year four and just two six months apart in year five.

She had already told me I was too weak to work that summer and said that my commentary career would need to be put on hold for some time, but I had to ease myself back into life in other ways. So I started accepting invitations to public events, something I had not normally done. If people were shocked when they saw me and how I looked, they were generally very kind and did not show it.

Rachael is also a good cook and loves entertaining, so for the first time in my life, having all this spare time on my hands meant we could start inviting friends over for lunch on a regular basis. On 26 April we had Fred Trueman and his wife Veronica, Richard and Allison Knaggs along with Martin Edwards and his then wife Sue.

Martin is a huge cricket fan and idolised Fred, but had never met him. You always worried with Fred whether he would take the story-telling too far, as he could show off in front of new people, but this day he was absolutely brilliant. He turned up in his big Rolls-Royce and had his dog with him, which he tied to a pear tree in our back garden. Throughout lunch he regaled us with stories for three hours about Len Hutton captaining in the West Indies, tales of Denis Compton, how quick Frank Tyson could bowl, and the day he met Harold Larwood.

He told Martin about meeting the 'three Ws' – Frank Worrell, Clyde Walcott and Everton Weekes – and how he had bowled to the great George Headley in his final Test on the 1953 tour to the West Indies. It was an outstanding performance from Fred, and he interspersed the cricketing tales with funny everyday jokes, but he never swore once and the girls were mesmerised by him. The funniest moment was when he just threw in the comment: 'And there's Len out on the balcony, giving this black girl one.' Martin's face was a picture when he replied to Fred: 'What! Sir Leonard?' He looked as if his boyhood dreams had just been shattered.

I was still exceptionally weak so in order to improve my fitness, I started Pilates classes most days at a gym in Wakefield. Rachael still needed to drive me, so said she would join in and keep an eye on me. Now she has always hated doing any exercise, but her idea was that she would get a flat stomach from the Pilates and I would get some muscles back. The instructor would give us exercises and stretching to do every day. It was as much as I could handle, because my muscles and ligaments had not been used for six months. It was funny though after a couple of weeks, when I got the flat stomach and Rachael the muscles, she decreed me well enough to drive myself and quit. I, on the other hand, really enjoyed it and my overall strength began to improve. My star nurse would still pop in to check up on me, and on 7 May we invited for tea the two ladies from the register office, Christine Smith and Norma Stroud, as a thank you for their help.

Later that month, I accepted an invitation for Rachael and me to be guests of the MCC at Lord's to watch a day of the Test match between England and Zimbabwe. This was my first cricket engagement since the cancer had been diagnosed. I was now back on familiar ground and if anyone asked about the cancer, I was honest but did not go into too much detail. It was a lovely time reconnecting with old friends but I got tired very quickly. The talking and travelling drained me and I soon wanted to go home.

The monthly check-ups were mentally exhausting. In the week or so leading up to each one, I would be nervous, then after I'd had the results I could relax for a couple of weeks before the nerves would start all over again. I knew if the cancer came back, it would be very hard to beat for a second time. This dread of Catherine Coyle finding something at each clinic was always there. I was not fearful exactly, but I knew I was under the cosh. Just because you have gone through months of gruelling treatment and the medical profession has done its best, it does not guarantee you will live.

To give myself the best chance, I was continuing with the new diet and vitamin supplements. The feng shui master visited us again on Friday 30 May to check the house and ensure everything was aligned properly. I needed as much reassurance as I could get and was always searching for diversions. As Rachael said, in reality I was bored so she got out hundreds of black and white pictures of my playing career and suggested I write on the back the date, venue and name of anyone else on the picture and then file them away in order of the year. She joked that way they would be worth more when I was dead.

A few weeks later, on 19 June, I was asked to appear on *This Is Your Life* for Alec Stewart. I liked Alec and had great respect for him. I always admired his professionalism and the fastidious care he took over his appearance. He should have got more recognition for his wicketkeeping, as he missed very little, and he was also a bloody good batsman on the front or back foot. To be honest I didn't really want to go all that way down to London for the show, but for him I made the effort. None of my suits fitted me and were all hanging off my skinny frame, but we managed to find one that was just about presentable. Even though they put me on last, it was still very exhausting and a reminder for me not to run before I could walk, but I was glad we went.

Towards the end of the month who should come for lunch but my great friend Brian Clough and his wife Barbara. He'd decided to come see for himself how I was. Brian was in good form, always interesting and made me laugh.

Throughout this period I had received many press requests for interviews. The late Lynda Lee Potter, of the *Daily Mail*, was one journalist who kept in constant touch, particularly with Rachael. I agreed she could actually come to my home to have an exclusive interview. I did not request any money. Lynda was charming but it was dangerous to underestimate her; she always gave me the impression that she was like that delightful Miss Marple from St Mary Mead. Lynda had a sharp brain taking everything in and quickly worked out the secret of my strength and always used to write: 'The great cricketer is lucky to have married Rachael.' Well as you can imagine, Rachael loved that. I still tease her even now, that she is lucky I married her.

By July I had started to write copy myself for my column in the *Daily Telegraph*. Rachael and I got our first invite to Fred's house for lunch, along with Brian Close, his wife Vivian and Ray Illingworth and wife Shirley. Now who would have believed that a few years earlier, during all the troubles between us. I had never been to the Truemans' house and found they had this gorgeous cottage with a beautiful garden overlooking the Yorkshire Dales. Fred was keen on birdlife and used to sit watching the birds from his lounge. There was a lot more to Fred Trueman than people think.

For some time, Mark Nicholas had been pressing me to give an interview on Channel 4 television about my recovery, but I was reluctant to do it as I did not want to tempt fate. I still had a long way to go and didn't know if I was going to live or die. People also get confused between 'in remission' and 'being cured', and I was still only in the first stage. However, feeling physically and mentally stronger in myself, I agreed to do a live interview with Mark during the Leeds Test match. I also gave one to Sky TV and to Jonathan Agnew on BBC's *Test Match Special*.

I did not realise it at the time, but this was the start of my getting on with my working life again. In September, I was asked by ESPN to fly to India for some promotional work, and when Catherine Coyle said it would be okay to go, I was happy to repay them for their continued support. I started in Delhi and had a three-hour session with the Indian media, which was like a rugby scrum. There were ten times more cameras than you would see at a press conference in England. I was also taken to visit a cancer hospital, then did shows with Sunil Gavaskar in Delhi and Calcutta. I ended up going to Singapore, where Rachael and Emma joined me, and did a programme in the ESPN studio talking about Sachin Tendulkar. It was a public relations exercise which I was thrilled to do and be a part of. I loved it all, finally arriving home on 31 October.

The next few weeks saw me gradually increase my workload almost back up to normal levels. I attended the opening of the ECB's Cricket Academy at Loughborough University and even had to stand in for the Queen, who was running late and helped fill in the time before her arrival by doing a question and answer session with Jonathan Agnew.

Two days later, we went over to Thorp Arch, near Wetherby, to the training ground of Leeds United Football Club. Jonny Bairstow was playing for Leeds Under-15s and I went to see how he played. Rachael had become very close to his mother Janet, after her husband David's death in January 1998 and we had looked out for her and closely watched young Jonny and his sister Becky grow up ever since. Janet was concerned that Jonathan was doing too much: he was playing rugby for Yorkshire schools, training for Yorkshire cricket's academy side and playing football for Leeds United. She asked me to have a word with him, but before that I needed to satisfy myself how he performed in all these sports. I told him he needed to give up one winter sport, in order to do justice to the other two. Which sport? He must decide which he liked the least, and football was the answer.

I left for Australia on 29 November for my first commentary gig since the cancer diagnosis. ESPN were covering the

Australia–India series and they promised me I could come off air at any time if I felt tired; it was a wonderful trip and I felt alive again. I was careful to avoid anyone with a runny nose, or a cold. My immune system took another two years to recover, so I was very wary of catching a virus and kept up the old Vaseline trick as a matter of course every morning.

Rachael and Emma came over for the Christmas holidays and we attended the famous Carols by Candlelight service in Melbourne on Christmas Eve, which Tony Greig had organised tickets for. This sort of thing would never have interested me before, but it was quite magical being able to watch the wonder and delight on my daughter's face. For New Year, we stayed at the Park Hyatt hotel in Sydney, overlooking Circular Quay and had a great view for the New Year's Eve fireworks, another poignant moment because I had not been sure I would make it so far as to see in another new year.

Catherine Coyle had agreed to my trip only if I agreed to see another oncologist for my check-ups, so I arranged to visit a Dr Patrick Bridger in Bankstown, Sydney. He had a look down my throat and reported all looked well and I could carry on with the rest of the tour, finally arriving home on 10 February. It was a long trip but I got through it with a bit of common sense and help from ESPN.

Over the next four years, I went to see Catherine for my check-ups and she would poke her fingers down my throat. It never got any easier. Sitting there waiting for the verdict is like waiting for the umpire to put up his finger or say not out. I was lucky that she always said not out, which was an enormous relief.

For my last two visits, after Cookridge had closed down, I had to report to St James Hospital in Leeds. On my penultimate visit, Catherine was looking down my throat and poking around and said: 'Right! I will see you in six months and that will be your last check-up.' I was just going out the door and she said: 'By the way, it is getting close now you know.' And with that, she tapped her bottom. I had promised her at the start of my treatment, I would kiss her arse if she saved me and she hadn't forgotten. She said the nurses would be ready with their cameras. She not only helped save my life, but she did it with humour and I liked her and will always be grateful.

As Mr Li, the feng shui master, predicted, I went on to celebrate my 70th birthday and invited 70 guests. Catherine Coyle was first on the list, but unfortunately was away attending an important conference. After her name came Pat Bradley, the surgeon from Nottinghamshire and his wife, and also guardian angel nurse Julie Maltman, who in fact with her husband had become a regular guest at our home parties and they all came to help me celebrate.

I am always asked if cancer changed me. I don't think anybody can totally change what they are and the characteristics of their DNA and personality. I'd always been a strident individual, forthright and frank, and you can't totally change that, but I think cancer does smooth off a lot of the edges.

Feng shui also believes you are born with characteristics common to that year. Funnily enough Rachael, Emma and I were all born in a dragon year. The only difference is I am a 'metal' dragon, which means I am strong and determined; Emma is an 'earth' dragon and has a mind 'like a platinum bear trap' and is if anything even more strong-minded than me, but also has some of her mum's way with people. Fortunately for both of us, Rachael was born a 'water' dragon, which means like water, she will always find a way through and solve any problem. But if she gets really cross, which happens about five times a year, Emma and I both know to run.

Surviving cancer doesn't stop you getting angry or mad sometimes, but Rachael gave me the best advice which pops into my mind today whenever I lose my temper. She just said: 'Say to yourself: does it really matter?' That is the most important thing. Does it matter if someone cuts across in front of me in their car, or my hotel room is not ready or there is a confused telephone receptionist when I ring up to speak to someone? OK, I still feel anger but it subsides quicker now.

I have been lucky to have spent an extra 12 years of life with my wife and daughter and would rather like at least another 12, but if I die tomorrow I have had the pride of seeing that 14-year-old girl grow up into a beautiful young woman, qualify as a litigation lawyer and start her own Wedding and Events consultancy business. The medical profession are saving a lot of people and performing wonders, but unfortunately more people are contracting this disease and it is like trying to hold back the tide: you can only do so much, as it keeps on coming.

A cure doesn't seem any nearer, and as a cancer survivor you can never declare you have beaten it, or as we say in Yorkshire, licked it. It could come back any time. I am one of the lucky ones. I have been given a few extra years and I have learned to enjoy every single minute of life. Don't waste it, because you don't know how long you have got on this earth. It may be a lot less than three score and ten years.

I know some people will laugh and be sceptical, but I truly believe that following all the different routes I did, and continuing with some even today, helped to save me from cancer. I will never know why I am still alive. Was it Catherine Coyle and her NHS treatment? Was it the feng shui or Chris Woollams and Patrick Kingsley's knowledge and complementary medicine? Was it fate or was it a combination of all those things? Who knows? The only thing I really do know for certain is I would not have survived without my wife Rachael being there for me.

CHAPTER 6

EXPLODING THE PACKER MYTH

Cancer afflicts one in three people, and many of my friends have fought their own battles. Tony Greig was one of them, and he was diagnosed with lung cancer just two months before he died in Sydney of a heart attack at the age of 66 in December 2012.

Six months later, I went to his UK memorial service at St Martin-in-the-Fields Church in Trafalgar Square. It was a wonderful setting, with eulogies delivered by Richie Benaud, Dennis Amiss, Michael Holding and David Gower. The whole occasion was organised by the England and Wales Cricket Board in accordance with his widow Vivian's instructions, a final sign that Tony had been accepted by the English cricketing establishment he had battled for so long.

Benaud and Amiss spoke warmly of Tony the man, but of

course World Series Cricket and his ties to Kerry Packer were never far away. More than 30 years had passed since that terribly divisive time, and a new gloss put on the civil war, sparked by Packer and Greig, that gripped cricket between 1976 and 1978.

The memorial service was a chance to reflect on Tony's life in a celebratory, happy way. But unfortunately there was an awful lot of twaddle written and spoken about the Packer issue, and I left the service feeling angry that history had been rewritten by people who were not involved in the events at the time. The eulogies made Tony out to be a saint who saved cricketers from poverty and the clutches of over-bearing, controlling administrators.

It started when I picked up the order of service. There was a piece by Mike Atherton, reproduced from his column in *The Times*, which trotted out the same old guff about how Packer improved the lives of modern-day players. I like Mike's writing, but on this occasion he never told us how or gave us any specifics. He wrote: 'Every cricketer who has made even a half-decent living from the game since then owes Greig and his contemporaries a debt of gratitude for the battle won against the rapacious administrators of three decades ago.'

Rubbish! How could he know? He has no first-hand knowledge, as he was nine years old at the time of Packer. He fell into the same trap as a lot of people by thinking Greig and Packer were the saviours of our game, but I don't see it that way.

Tony's widow, Vivian, gave a long-winded lecture which made me want to stand up and leave. She hardly mentioned anything at all about Tony the man, the guy she married and what fun company he could be. Instead she appeared to want to settle a score in London against the British Establishment over Packer and World Series Cricket. She made him out to be an altruistic man who gave up the captaincy of England to benefit cricketers everywhere and suggested that we were all indebted to him. I sat there thinking: 'No, this is not right.' I found it sick-making. It was very far from my own experience of those times.

I wondered what Vivian could possibly know about those events. She was 17 at the time, so she can know only what Tony or the other World Series cricketers have told her. Over the years, she spent many hours at my house and I at hers and Packer cricket was never raised once by any of us. She, like Mike Atherton, had no personal knowledge of it, so they can't possibly comprehend the emotion and bitterness involved. They can have no idea of the resentment I felt sat there in the church about their version of events. At the time, you were either for or against Packer cricket; people became very entrenched in their views and it was a very unpleasant two-year period for the game, and we shouldn't pretend otherwise.

Packer touched upon issues of nationality and loyalty, for the players who signed up, and in particular for Tony Greig, and for those who didn't. The result was that it set friend against friend, as happened with Tony and me, and that is why it remains such a powerful issue to this day.

At the heart of the matter was a domineering giant of a man in Packer. Greigy, a flamboyant character who shared his new boss's ruthless ability to pursue his own agenda, was also a key figure in the story. It ended up in a High Court case and many of the people involved do not look back on it fondly. As each side tried to get its view heard, I ended up spending hours being cross-examined in the witness box, was rubbished in the press by Tony, and accused of pulling out of Packer cricket in a sulk over not being offered the captaincy. I was smeared and it hurt, but it was all rubbish. Tony, Kerry Packer and those who worked for him did a fantastic PR job making people believe their actions would change cricketers' lives for the better. But it wasn't like that.

I believe the whole Packer circus can be traced back to a blank winter for England in 1975–76. Tony had been made England captain earlier that year and, with no winter tour, he got an opportunity out of the blue to go to Australia to play for Waverley Cricket Club, near Bondi Beach in Sydney. He was not paid any money to play cricket, but the club said it would find him work and he would turn out for them as an amateur.

It was not hard to find him employment as Tony was not only a celebrity in 1970s Sydney, he had a huge personality and presence. He was made for television and this was spotted by one of the Waverley members, a man named Ian Macfarlane, who worked in advertising. He soon fixed him up with television contracts, a newspaper column and lots of commercial work. Tony loved it. He was perfect for it and he played absolutely fabulously for Waverley on Saturdays. He gained respect for his performances and made many friends. It laid the groundwork for what was to follow in 1977.

Before England left for India in late 1976, Tony had a couple of free months after the end of the season, which allowed him to have another quick trip to Sydney to do more television work and personal appearances. He did not play for Waverley this time and made the trip for purely commercial reasons. It was financially rewarding and a tremendous fillip for his ego.

You have to remember that in England in the 1970s, it was very difficult for sportsmen to find work in television advertising, or product endorsement. Actors and actresses took almost all the available spots. The actors' union, Equity, looked after its people very well and it was hard for cricketers, or any other sportsmen, to get a look-in. However, in Australia they did not have as many showbiz stars, so sportsmen were in greater demand, and Tony was able to cash in. If you were good, they idolised you and gave you opportunities. Sydney also offered sea, sunshine and a beautiful city, just what he had grown up with in South Africa. He felt very comfortable there and it gave him ideas for the future.

While he was on this trip, he recommended me to Waverley Cricket Club, as I wasn't playing for England at the time through my own choice. During this period, I spent quite a bit of time with Tony and his first wife Donna, and I would join them at their house where she would frequently cook for us both. I had first-hand knowledge of what he was thinking, and believe that this adventure into the commercial world of television made a big impact on him and changed his outlook on life, leading to massive consequences for the rest of us.

In the winter of 1976–77, while I was playing for Waverley, having taken Greigy's place, the same man who helped Tony, Ian Macfarlane, sorted me out with media work. I had two newspaper columns, with the *Sydney Daily Telegraph* and the *Sydney Morning Herald*, and TV commentary work with the 0-10 Network commentating on Sheffield Shield cricket.

I would have nets at Waverley on the Thursday then fly to

somewhere like Brisbane or Melbourne to commentate on the state game on the Friday. I would return to Sydney on Friday night and play for Waverley the following day. After I'd played, I would fly back to commentate on the end of the Shield game. The club also gave me a lovely battered old second-hand car and I had a fantastic time.

In January 1977 John Spencer of Sussex, who was coaching in Sydney, told me Kerry Packer would like me to go and look at his son. Kerry had a net in his back garden and I went to see young James bat. He was about nine years old and was a nice little batsman, but Kerry would not stop interrupting. The kid was nervous and always looking at his dad for approval while I was coaching him. Kerry was too overbearing and that is not good for kids, as it makes them concentrate more on pleasing Dad than on learning batting. I made him turn his back on his father, talk to me and listen to my advice not his dad's. Then his father said: 'I don't want him to be a professional cricketer because they don't earn anything.' It made me wonder why he'd asked me to go there.

I thought that would be the end with Kerry Packer, but soon after John Spencer said that Packer wanted to see me again, and this time it was about a coaching job for the following season. As I was a free agent in the winter months, I went to his offices in Sydney on Tuesday 8 March, just before the Centenary Test in Melbourne, and he said if I returned to Australia the following year he could give me a job coaching cricket in the territories outside the big cities of Australia. He asked what I would want financially and when I told him £20,000 to take on the role, he refused to pay that, so I got up to walk out. As I was about to leave, he said: 'Just a minute.

I have something else I want to talk to you about, but I need your assurance that whatever happens you will keep it confidential.'

He said he was going to put together some cricket matches in the next Australian season between a World XI and an Australian XI, which would include some of the players who had just retired such as Ian Chappell, Ross Edwards and Ian Redpath. Australia were due to play India that season, and he felt it would not be of much interest to the Australian public. He asked if I would be interested in playing for his World XI? I said yes, as I was hoping to come back anyway and play for Waverley in the English winter.

I had no idea he was setting himself up to go against established cricket, and I had no knowledge of his meeting with the Australian Cricket Board nine months earlier in June 1976, when he was refused the opportunity to bid for the Australian television cricket rights. How could I know this was the start of his scheming and plotting to get top-class cricket on his television station Channel 9? I also did not know this was a man not used to being turned down or not getting his own way. Only later did I realise all this, and that to Kerry money equalled power.

I thought he was going to sign players for exhibition matches, like the Rothmans International Cavaliers, who had played 40 overs per side on Sundays during the English summer. I had played for them a few times, and their sides tended to consist of current English players plus some already retired big-name players such as Denis Compton, Ted Dexter and Godfrey Evans. These matches were shown on BBC TV and big crowds came along.

There was no entrance fee allowed because of the Sunday observance laws at the time, which also meant there was no county or international cricket on that day, so instead a collection would be taken by passing a big blanket around the crowd. The counties got around it by letting in only those spectators who had first bought a programme or scorecard outside the ground. These games were essentially the forerunners of 40-over county cricket, which started in 1969. The counties, having seen how lucrative and popular these matches were, wanted some of it for themselves. When I spoke to Packer, this was what I thought he had in mind. Clearly he had bigger ambitions.

To put it in perspective, at that time there had never been a private promoter to challenge established cricket. So how could I realise the enormity of what he was proposing and its consequences? Perhaps I was naive but I never grasped his intentions.

He then began to pick my brains about the best players in the world and about the captaincy. I thought he meant captains outside the established Test teams, and that is why I recommended Raymond Illingworth. He had been the best captain I had played under and although he had lost the England job in 1973 he was still skipper of Leicestershire. More to the point, like me, he was not playing international cricket and would therefore be available. It was when Packer dismissed Illy's name that I put myself forward. Why not me? I was captain of Yorkshire and had always wanted to be captain of England, but it had not happened. If I had realised for a moment that it was his intention to sign up the best players in the world, I would not have stupidly embarrassed myself by putting my name up in front of guys like Clive Lloyd, Mushtaq Mohammad, Imran Khan and Tony Greig, who were already international captains.

Kerry asked me if I was commentating at the Centenary Test match, and I told him they had already got a full quota of commentators but I was going as an invited guest of the Australia Cricket Board, along with other former players. He asked if I would like to commentate and I said yes. He made two phone calls and informed me I would be offered a role. That is how powerful he was, and I just took it as a thank you for coaching his son or maybe the information I had just given him. I left the meeting having agreed he would send me a contract to play for him during the following winter.

Austin Robertson, a former Aussie Rules footballer who worked for Packer, came to see me during the Centenary Test in Melbourne and he showed me the official contract, which was huge. There were a lot of pages which involved selling your body and soul for 12 months over three years, with 11 clauses that gave Packer control over your cricket life.

I asked if I could take it away to show my solicitor in England, but he would not let me. He said that secrecy was the reason I could not have a copy, but added that he was coming to England soon to sign up players and to scout for suitable grounds where they could play matches in the future. I told him I could not sign the contract, as I knew enough about legal matters to understand that I already had a contract in existence to play for Yorkshire from 1 April until the end of September, so how could I sign for somebody else? I could just imagine what would happen if Yorkshire had taken me, their captain, to court.

When they later tried to discredit me, I was accused by Kerry Packer and Tony Greig of turning down the contract because I was not going to be the captain. That's nonsense because Packer told me at our meeting I was only the third player to be approached, so nobody could know who was going to sign up for him or what the team would be. I also did not turn it down because I didn't like Kerry Packer or because the money was not enough, because no sum was ever discussed. I never heard anything more from him about a possible role and did not even give it another thought.

We later learnt that a few days after the Centenary Test match, Tony Greig had gone to see Packer in Sydney. I can only guess that through his exposure to the Sydney business world, he must have realised it was an opportunity of a lifetime to talk to Packer, especially for a man like Tony who was always trying to work out how to maximise his earnings from cricket. He gathered straight away what the opportunity entailed and I believe he jumped at it. Maybe he was given a lot more information than me, or perhaps the fact I refused to sign led Packer to offer more incentives.

I don't believe he went into this meeting thinking he would throw away the England captaincy and help set up a rebel cricket tournament. He probably just wanted to earn a few quid, but in life opportunities do not always come at a time convenient to you. Tony was like a lot of cricketers, once you reach 30 you start to worry about the future and how you would pay the bills after retirement. Packer was offering some players a guaranteed £25,000 per year for three years, which was a huge amount at the time, so you can see why they would want to sign up.

To give you an idea of how much it was, when I rejoined the England team in July 1977 at Trent Bridge for the third Test against Australia, I was paid the princely sum of £400 for the week's work. If you played in all five Tests you would get £2,000. However, it wasn't guaranteed the selectors would choose you for every game and central contracts were a distant dream, so the money could easily be less than that. If you were selected for an England tour then you would get approximately £5,000. On top of that, my salary at Yorkshire was £3,000 to £4,000.

If you were a star player or captain of England, you could pick up odd bits and pieces to improve your income. However, if you wrote a newspaper column, it had to be shown to and approved by the Test and County Cricket Board (TCCB, the forerunner of the ECB). The articles were censored to prevent you from publishing any critical comments, which meant the newspapers were not going to pay very much money for copy that did not make headlines. The *Sun* newspaper paid me because my name carried some interest, but that was it.

Nowadays players earn a lot of money from sponsorship, but there were also strict rules in those days around bat advertising. The rules stated you could have only a bat maker's name on the back of your cricket bat, rather than a company or sponsor. It was a closed shop. Bat makers such as Gunn & Moore, Gray-Nicolls, Stuart Surridge, County Sports and Slazenger had us all by the balls. You got a couple of grand and some free kit – that was it.

As a result of my 100th first-class century at Headingley in the fourth Test, I became the first player to earn serious money from bat sponsorship. I negotiated a £9,000 per year guarantee, with a per centage of sales which meant I could earn up to £12,000 or £13,000 a year. It was an unheard-of sum of money. Nowadays Kevin Pietersen or MS Dhoni can earn hundreds of thousands of pounds from bat sponsorships alone.

If you added up all my cricket and bat sponsorship contracts, the money still did not equal what was on offer from Packer. And, as I later told the High Court, there was another vital difference: players did not have the security of contracts. As I mentioned earlier, at Yorkshire we had only a yearly agreement until I negotiated contracts in 1972. The club would write to me and say it was employing me for a year and then they specified the salary. I had no security as an England player either, as what money there was depended on my being selected to play.

The contrast was stark. In the summer of 1977, as the Packer story swirled around the game, the TCCB were shamed into giving us a pay rise. A businessman named David Evans and some of his friends offered to increase the England players' wages to £1,000 per match, meaning we were paid an extra £600 a Test if we did not sign with Packer. The money went to the TCCB who then passed it on to us, minus the tax.

It embarrassed the TCCB that someone else had to help pay our wages and the following year, partly out of the fear more players would defect to World Series Cricket, they did then pay us £1000 per match out of their own money. So, in a very small way, Packer did improve wages for Test match players that summer, but it was hardly a life-changing sum of money and we still had no guarantees that we would keep on receiving the money.

Just look at what happened to me the following year in 1978. I was a top player and still good enough to be picked at 37, but

I missed four Test matches (three against Pakistan and one against New Zealand) through injury after breaking my thumb fielding for England in a one-day international against Pakistan. I played just two Tests that summer, so instead of earning £6,000 I received only £2,000, even though I had been injured while playing for my country. You can see why cricketers were easy pickings for Packer. He found a group of men who were ready to sell out because they felt they had been underpaid for years.

Where money is involved, arguments soon follow and the controversy and backbiting started in May 1977 when the Packer story broke. It did not take long for me to be dragged into it and become a target. I first got wind of the storm brewing when Yorkshire played Sussex at Hove on Sunday 8 May. Sussex beat us by five wickets and Greigy won the match with 50 not out. As I was about to drive off, Tony suggested I join him for a drink in the pub. This was not something I would normally do, as pubs were not for me and so I declined.

Tony then advised me to have a look at the papers the following morning as the story was about to break that he had signed for Packer, along with a lot more players. I was amazed but it did not particularly bother me, as I still did not realise what it was all about or the enormous implications for cricket. How could I?

On my way back to Chesterfield for a Yorkshire match next day, I called in to see Greigy's wife, Donna, to thank her for being so kind to me when I had been in Sydney playing for Waverley the previous winter. Richard Lumb and Bill Athey were in my car and they also came into the house with me. This meeting would later take on importance to the Packer circus.

The next day all hell broke loose. The story about Packer and World Series Cricket was all over the papers, and every day after that Greigy was making statements, holding press conferences, going on television, trying to explain why he signed and why other players had signed up. He told the world how it would benefit cricket and cricketers, though how was never made clear. Packer was also making statements from Australia, explaining how he was basically pissed off that he had not been allowed to bid for television rights for Australian cricket.

A lot of normally gentle, good-natured, easygoing people were upset. They felt Tony had let English cricket down, the more so because as England captain he had become Packer's recruiting sergeant. He would have been better relinquishing the captaincy and then doing what he did. Alec Bedser said at the time: 'The secretive, clandestine manner in which the opposition to traditional cricket was set up with the English captain acting as a recruiting agent left a mixture of numbing sadness and anger.'

But secrecy had been paramount; Packer had insisted on it. If Tony had given up the England captaincy at the peak of his powers, as he was in 1977, the press would have sniffed out World Series Cricket, so he had to carry out this clandestine recruitment process that added to the poisonous atmosphere at the time.

Once the news was out, every day there was so much conjecture as to who had signed or who was going to be approached. There was talk of a conciliation meeting between Packer's people and the International Cricket Council (ICC), then called the International Cricket Conference. It started to become bitter and a lot of hurtful comments were made by both sides aimed at various individuals. Once it became public knowledge that Tony had been recruiting players to sign for Kerry Packer, the TCCB had no alternative but to take the England captaincy away from him. How can you be a senior manager for Tesco and yet be recruiting people for Sainsbury's? It was ludicrous.

Rumours were rife, because no one knew who had the correct information, and once Tony lost the England captaincy, he jumped in with all guns blazing having realised his whole life was now going to be with Packer and away from established cricket. He was like a salesman trying to convince everyone, or maybe just convince himself, he had done the right thing, and that this was going to be the salvation for cricketers.

Fact became fiction. The Packer team twisted everything to suit their side of things and there was a PR war raging. In my case, Tony told *Private Eye* that when I went to his house to see Donna, I had actually gone in alone and waited for him to come home. I had then pleaded with him to ring Packer on my behalf, as I had changed my mind and wanted to come on board. Tony went on to say in the article that he had done this, but Packer did not want to know. It was a pack of lies to discredit me. He was under so much pressure and criticism in trying to justify his own actions he got carried away and seemed to have no conscience.

The Packer saga was in full swing, and Dennis Amiss, Derek Underwood, Alan Knott and John Snow had all signed up. On 26 July 1977, the ICC issued a statement saying: 'No player who, after 1 October 1977, has played or has made himself available to play in a match previously disapproved by the conference shall be eligible to play in any Test.'

This was a warning to all players that if they signed for World Series Cricket they were going to be banned from established cricket. Both sides had tried in a meeting at Lord's on 23 June to resolve the issue and hammer out an agreement, without success. After the meeting Packer was angry, saying: 'I will take no steps at all to help anybody. From now on it is every man for himself and let the devil take the hindmost.'

Talk now started that anyone playing for Packer would also be banned from county cricket the following season. This is when Packer started legal action, as he believed that the restrictions suggested by the ICC and TCCB were unlawful. I was asked to be a witness in the High Court for the TCCB, a shock to say the least. They actually wanted me on their side for a change. I was not used to being considered one of the good guys. By then, news of my rejection of Packer had circulated worldwide and I was regarded as public enemy number one by him and Tony. As soon as it became clear I was to give evidence, Tony telephoned me to ask: 'How the hell have you got involved in this?' He then added: 'We'll have to work hard over the weekend to find some mud to throw at you.'

That Sunday we met at the Sports Fair in Birmingham, he had to appear for St Peter's and I for Slazenger. He repeated his remark about finding something to have a go at me with the next day in court. Presumably he had already forgotten the despicable story he had earlier circulated, accusing me of asking him to contact Packer to get me in on the team, when I had visited his home in Sussex. Surely had that been true, it would have been brought up in court. You can always remember the truth, but you forget what lies you have told.

The judge, on being apprised of Tony's remark that they

would have to find some mud to discredit me, decided that his words were only jocular and satisfied legal dignity with a warning.

At the High Court on Monday 17 September, I was cross-examined by Packer's lawyer for nearly four hours. They quizzed me on the contractual situation of county cricketers, the problems they faced in gaining employment in the winter and my view on whether Packer players should be able to represent England. I was clear on that point. 'If a man feels he can earn more money by going away and playing in another country in direct conflict or opposition with the already established cricketers, then it is fine for him to do that. He has to earn his living. But he can't come back to the same system that is pouring money in left, right and centre not just to keep a few cream players happy but to keep the whole game going. These players surely can't expect to go and earn a lot of money and then come back and play in the established game. It seems nonsense.'

Mr Justice Slade found against the ICC and the TCCB, ruling that their action amounted to an illegal restraint of trade. The High Court judgement did however leave a loophole. While he had made it impossible for the authorities to ban the 'rebels' from any form of the professional game, a good deal of power still remained in the hands of the Test selectors and county committees. They could dispense with the services of any individual on the basis of form or team spirit, which is so often a matter of opinion.

The Professional Cricketers' Association, formed in 1968, came out strongly against Packer almost immediately, voting that his recruits should be ousted from the County

Championship. They showed an impressive solidarity which persuaded me to join their ranks after I had ignored their existence for nine years, in the belief the PCA was little more than a talking shop. In the end, player power probably did more than anything else to preserve established cricket, a factor that came to prominence when I finally became captain of England in 1978.

Bearing in mind the way the fates have sometimes treated me, I should not really have been surprised to find myself captain and having to face the possibility of a strike by the England team over Packer players. Mike Brearley, the captain of the tour to Pakistan in the winter of 1977–78, broke his arm in a meaningless fixture at Lahore, so I stepped in to deputise in the third Test at Karachi on 18 January. In doing so I picked up a poisoned chalice.

Whatever the High Court's view, all concerned with the England party were under the impression that Packer players would not be selected during our three-match Test series, although the Pakistan authorities had lifted the ban on their five rebels and invited four of them – Mushtaq Mohammad, Majid Khan, Zaheer Abbas and Imran Khan – to join their squad. The fifth, Asif Iqbal, indicated that he would not be available and dropped out of the picture.

Initially, however, it appeared that this represented little more than a gesture by the Pakistani authorities, as our Test series clashed with the so-called Super Test fixtures Packer had arranged. It was reported that the five Pakistani stars had turned down an offer of around £270 per Test from their board. Majid spotlighted the dangers of the deteriorating situation when he admitted: 'I am always available for selection unless

I am under contract to someone else at the same time.' In other words, he was happy to let Packer dictate his programme, a point Mushtaq underlined when he pressed the Pakistani board to negotiate with the Australian.

People's suspicions increased when Mushtaq, Zaheer and Imran flew in to Karachi. Their arrival on the scene indicated the distinct probability that Pakistan were going to include them in their line-up for this final Test. The entire England party was against contact with the Packer trio and the degree of uncertainty in the Pakistan camp prompted Brearley, on his return to England, to voice our opposition. 'The lads were not scared of being beaten, but worried about the future and wanted to make it quite clear where they stand. They are unanimously opposed to Packer's players being considered for selection in ICC Tests.'

To a large extent, Brearley did no more than hint at the depth of feeling in the England camp, and his words emphasised his unease at any talk of a strike, but, putting it bluntly, England were not prepared to take the field against any Packer players and industrial action represented the most effective option. I had a mess to sort out.

Meanwhile, a good deal was going on behind the scenes. Cricket officials in Pakistan are wary of their public, who they worried might riot, cause trouble and virtually wreck the ground if their favourite personalities were not picked, and the would-be spectators on this occasion were certainly not interested in the complications of politics. Those running the game in Pakistan were under just as much pressure as the players, so we appreciated that nothing could be taken for granted. We had to plan our strategy in the knowledge that the Pakistan selectors could not afford to be seen to be backing down by not picking their players. They were trapped between the proverbial rock and a hard place.

Doug Insole, chairman of the TCCB, sent an urgent telegram from London to the Intercontinental Hotel, where we were staying, which read: 'Messrs Barrington and Boycott, please ring me any time after 0300 your time.' Ken Barrington was the tour manager but he didn't really know how to cope with such a dramatic turn of events. He was a fine, determined player and a good man on the cricket side, but in his managerial role Ken preferred to distance himself from this sort of turmoil.

Insole's concern centred on the legal position, as he thought Pakistan could sue the TCCB for a substantial sum if we did not play, so he stressed to me: 'It would be bad for England and it would be bad for you, as history will record that you were the captain and Barrington the manager. Those are the two names that will be remembered. Surely you don't want that to happen. You are a responsible, mature person and I implore you, as a personal favour, to persuade the players to play.'

How ironic that the man who dropped me for slow scoring ten years earlier, when England beat India and I scored 246 not out, was now coming to me for help. He had publicly humiliated me and given me the stigma of scoring slowly that has lasted to this day. Now he wanted a personal favour. I wouldn't have given it to him even if it had been within my power.

I admitted that I did not feel it was up to me to dictate to the rest of the squad, adding that no words of mine would have the desired effect as feelings were running very high. The news of the solidarity in the England camp clearly surprised Insole, so

I tried to make him appreciate the position from our point of view. 'Look at Bob Taylor,' I said. 'If he were being selfish after getting the chance to step into Knott's shoes, he would want to play and keep his nose clean. Then he'd have a good chance of keeping his place next year. I've got most to lose. I have just realised my life's ambition to be captain of England, so it is not in my best interests to rock the boat. At the moment my prospects of taking over from Brearley would be improved if I were to toe the official line, but I don't operate like that. I am trying to do what I honestly believe is best for cricket.'

Insole listened without really hearing what I was saying. He continued to plead the case for appeasement. 'I take your point,' he admitted. 'We are all aware of your sentiments at Lord's, but you need to show some leadership. You can carry the rest of the team with you.'

That made me angry, because Insole was implying that to prove my qualities as captain I had to make a resolute England dressing room follow me against their clearly expressed better judgement. To leave no room for any doubt, therefore, I put several players on the telephone to Insole in the course of the ongoing discussions. The resulting exchanges reflected our collective distress at the circumstances in which we were placed through no fault of our own. Chris Old had turned down Packer to play for England and couldn't stomach the thought of them returning. Ian Botham and Bob Taylor felt this was a chance to make a stand after the failure of the TCCB's court case.

The conversation went round and round in circles and, having reached stalemate, I advised Insole to send the Pakistan board a telegram to cover the TCCB, which he did. It read: 'The UK Cricket Council warns your board England players adamant will not play Test if additional players from Australia are selected. Team has been instructed to play, but Cricket Council cannot guarantee them complying. If such players selected, consequences at Pakistan board's own risk.'

The England squad also received their 'instructions' in the same way: 'Following the phone call with the England captain, should players decide against playing the Cricket Council confirms the instructions that the England cricket team should fulfil their obligations to play the final Test match with Pakistan and honour both the board's contractual obligations and also those of the England players to the TCCB, despite whatever selections made by the Pakistan board for their side.'

The England party agreed to stand firm, and it is worth noting that we received total support for our decision from the Pakistan squad. Obviously some of them were motivated by self-interest, because if three Packer men were recalled at the last minute then three of the original side would have to be dropped, but the captain, Wasim Bari, was in no danger of losing his place and he too backed our position.

Then the Pakistan board president Mohammad Hussain announced that Mushtaq, Zaheer and Imran would not play. He insisted that the selectors had not bowed to any pressure from outside, but I am convinced that had the England players not stuck out their necks so loyally and bravely the rebels would have been welcomed back into the fold.

Another powerful voice, probably the most powerful of all, belonged to General Zia Ul-Haq, Pakistan's martial law administrator. He watched play during the first morning and asked me to visit him to give my views on the Packer circus and outline our version of events in the tense build-up to the Test. I went for tea with the general, along with Wasim Bari, and sought his opinion. He told me he was against the Packer trio being part of the Pakistan team, an opinion which certainly had reached the ears of the selectors, who must have looked to him for guidance, particularly as the fear of civil unrest hung over their deliberations. He added that he had spoken to Mushtaq and Zaheer.

Mushtaq and Zaheer must have departed in some haste after that, and General Zia clearly understood things perfectly. Both Wasim and I took the opportunity to emphasise that we did not want Packer men to be included in the Pakistan squad to tour England in the summer of 1978.

As England travelled on to New Zealand, the players' hard line became cemented into a series of resolutions put forward for consideration by the PCA, which included not playing first-class cricket against any touring side that selected players contracted to professional cricket outside the control of the ICC and TCCB. It was also put forward that members of the association would not play with or against players contracted to professional cricket outside the control of the ICC and TCCB in first-class cricket, John Player League, Benson & Hedges Cup and Gillette Cup while their contracts precluded their availability for Test matches and their own countries' domestic competitions.

I deliberately did not put my name to any proposal, as I did not want World Series Cricket and Tony to have any more ammunition. However, on behalf of the squad, I did write to Doug Insole to confirm our position, which we all felt was justified. If the England players had followed the TCCB line and featured in that Karachi Test alongside the Packer trio, Test

Early days, preparing for the start of the 1965 season, having made my international debut the previous summer.

My last innings. Going out to bat with Ashley Metcalfe at Scarborough on 10 September 1986 in my final game.

David Lloyd and I survey the pitch at Bramall Lane, Sheffield, on 4 August 1973 – the last first-class match to be played there. *(Getty Images)*

With two great friends, Dickie Bird and Michael Parkinson at Lord's in 2005, celebrating Michael's 70th birthday.

I was very proud to accept the role as Yorkshire president, but sadly there were some who tried to stir up trouble before I took on the job.

Bob Appleyard, me, Raymond Illingworth and Phil Sharpe during my time as president of Yorkshire CCC.

Brian Clough takes over at Leeds United, and I joined him soon after this picture was taken. How I wish he'd been my cricket coach, rather than the greatest manager English football has ever produced. *(Mirrorpix)*

Manchester United are my favourite team, ever since Denis Law signed for them in 1962. Here I am with Sir Bobby Charlton and Martin Edwards, president of the club.

On holiday in the Caribbean with Richard Knaggs and Tony Greig in 2004. Sadly, so much twaddle has been spoken about the Packer affair, in which Tony played such a central role.

It was at the Lamb Inn in Rainton where I met Rachael, the love of my life.

Our wedding day on 26 February 2003. Because of my battle with cancer, I had lost so much weight that my suit almost drowned me.

Our house near Paarl in South Africa, overlooking a Jack Nicklaus-designed golf course. I bought the plot of land when I was battling against cancer.

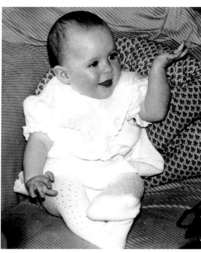

Like peas in a pod: me and my daughter Emma as babies.

Emma changed my life in so many ways, as I had to adapt to new responsibilities. Here she is encouraging me to try out a swimming pool. Strange as it may seem, I'd always avoided them in the past.

Dancing with Emma on my 70th birthday.

The Indian cricket team came to visit me in my house in Woolley just after I had discovered a lump in my neck.

LEFT: With my brother Tony, who helped me so much during my illness.

BELOW LEFT: When I saw this picture, and how thin I had become during my battle with cancer, I knew I had to do something to regain my strength.

BELOW RIGHT: The mask I had to put on when I was having my chemotherapy.
(Philip Brown)

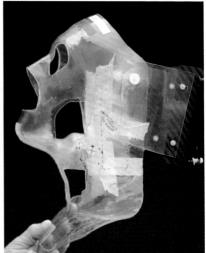

The curse of sledging is bringing down cricket. Here Michael Clarke confronts Jimmy Anderson during the Brisbane Test in November 2013. There was no excuse for what he said. *(Getty Images)*

It is crucial that Test cricket remains the pinnacle of the game – if it means adopting day/night matches with a pink ball to help draw in the crowds, I'm all for it. *(Getty Images)*

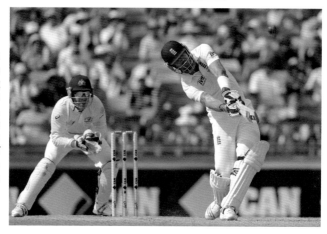

Kevin Pietersen tries to hit the ball for six during the Perth Test in December 2013, only to be caught on the boundary – it looked as if he did not give a damn. *(Getty Images)*

If England are to stand a chance in the Ashes series of 2015, they will have to learn how to handle the express pace of Mitchell Johnson. *(Getty Images)*

The new generation, with Joe Root among them, will play a vital role in next year's Ashes series. *(Getty Images)*

cricket would have had to accommodate the Packer circus and its players.

At the time of the Pakistan row, Tony Greig was miles away in Sydney and unable to restrain his frustration at the turn of events. Packer had released his Pakistan Test players as a PR exercise, and here was the England team putting a spanner in the works. Tony was so mad that in his weekly newspaper column he wrote 'The threatened strike is the work of Geoff Boycott and his cronies. I refuse to believe that Mike Brearley had anything to do with it. Boycott put the team up to this. Brearley insisted that I and the other Packer players should turn out for him and has always stood for compromise and no division.'

That may have been Brearley's stance in the summer, but once the ICC ban had come into effect in October even he could not have kept that same view. Tony was wrong if he imagined that Brearley could guarantee him, or any other Packer player, a welcome in the dressing room. There was now a ban in place regardless of who was captain, and Tony had not seemed to grasp that, or did not want to. Greig joined Doug Insole in mistakenly assuming I could control the England team and bend the players to my will.

Meanwhile, things were not going well in Australia. The Packer empire was not making the expected impact on the field at that time, crowds were poor, people were not turning up in great numbers to watch his players, and being charitable it may well have had Tony thinking: 'Have I made the right decision?' Because things were not going his way, Tony needed to hit out. As usual my name seemed the most likely to capture the headlines.

I suspect there was also a personal element to it all. Before the whole Packer episode, when Tony was captain of England for two years, he had tried to persuade me to play for him and I know it irked him that it never happened. Now I had not only turned Packer down, I had been a witness in the court case for the other side and here I was, captain of England. He could not hide his bitterness. He wrote: 'Boycott's ability to be where there were no fast bowlers was common knowledge in the game.'

This was a direct attack on me personally. He was saying I was afraid of fast bowling, citing as proof my absence from the 1974–75 tour to Australia, during which pace bowlers Dennis Lillee and Jeff Thomson destroyed England with their sustained hostility. His preposterous suggestion took no account of the facts. In early October 1974, when I made my decision to stay at home and not tour Australia that winter, hardly anyone had heard of Jeff Thomson, certainly not I or the rest of the England players. He had played one Test match, against Pakistan in Melbourne in December 1972, and finished with figures of none for 110 runs and as a consequence been dropped. He then spent 23 months in the wilderness and was a surprise choice for the first Test in Brisbane against England in November 1974.

Dennis Lillee had broken down with back trouble in the West Indies in February 1973 emerging from his last Test in Kingston, Jamaica, with none for 132. Nobody was sure if he was going to return to first-class cricket, never mind Test cricket, when the tour set off. So when he was selected for the first Test, he had also been off the scene for 21 months. It was only when England started collapsing against the ferocious fast bowling of Lillee and Thomson that my enemies started to say: 'Where's Boycott? England's best batsman should be here.'

But because I wasn't there and England were getting badly beaten, my critics started to fabricate malicious stories that I had made myself unavailable to tour Australia through the fear of top-notch fast bowling. Now, three years later, Greigy was repeating this myth in the hope of trying to hurt and discredit me. It was even more ridiculous this time, because only four months previously that summer I had just played with him in three Test matches in England against Australia, facing Jeff Thomson and Len Pascoe in full cry, and I managed to average 147 over five innings.

Two years later, when I was in my 40th year, I played five Test matches in England and four in the West Indies against the best fast bowling attack ever: Michael Holding, Andy Roberts, Joel Garner, Colin Croft and Malcolm Marshall, and I still averaged 40. Unfortunately, the more a lie is repeated the more it becomes fact and some people started to believe it, or hoped it was true. Even today this myth occasionally rears its head.

For Tony the end was nigh. He had been reappointed captain of Sussex for the 1978 summer, but this was in defiance of a private agreement between the counties to hold the future of the Packer men in abeyance. His personal attacks on me caused Sussex acute embarrassment. Lancashire and Nottinghamshire reacted most strongly, seeking to have Sussex expelled from the County Championship. They probably never expected to get backing for such an extreme step, however it did have the effect of Sussex sacking Greigy as their captain on 31 January 1978. As it transpired, he played only four more first-class matches in England and left the country to start a new life in Australia bitter at his treatment.

Was it worth all the fuss? When peace was finally brokered after two years of upheaval, did our wages improve at county or international level? No, did they hell. Tony had constantly tried to sell World Series Cricket to us all by insisting it would benefit every cricketer in the land, but that did not happen. Packer was the only one who won: he succeeded in the High Court case, and Channel 9 have shown Australian cricket for over 35 years. He got what he wanted and because of this there is a misconception that everything he said about helping all cricketers must have happened, and must be true.

There is no question that Packer won the battle, but that does not mean he improved the pay of all cricketers. The only cricketers he helped were the ones he signed up. The people who were to benefit were those who worked in and for World Series Cricket for two years, including players and umpires. Packer did nothing for the average county cricketer. The only pay rise we received was through those businessmen embarrassing the TCCB into upping our match fee.

What really did make the difference to wages? Television. Once the satellite television industry boomed in the 1990s, competition between the stations benefited the cricket authorities, who began to earn more for their TV rights. Sky, ESPN and other channels have created a market and it has rained money ever since.

To give you some idea of the scale of the change, in 1977, before Packer, the TCCB earned £1 million from radio and television rights from the BBC. The ECB's broadcasting contract with Sky from 2014 to 2017 is £337 million, an average of

£84 million per year. Television money started filtering down to the players, but it took another 20 years after Packer because it was not until 2006 that Sky finally owned the exclusive rights to England cricket and the millions started rolling in. Then along came the IPL in 2008 and that changed everything, making multi-millionaires of the top players.

In 1977 the TCCB were making only £200,000 per year from Cornhill in sponsorship. But if you have television, what comes after it? Sponsorship, marketing and perimeter board advertising at the grounds. In the 1980s, ground advertising started to become common for the first time. The non-Test match grounds received £13,000 and the Test grounds £100,000 per year. Most grounds still own that income stream today and the figures have increased by 500 per cent.

I saw this increased valuation with my own eyes. In 2000, I helped Kelvin MacKenzie and talkSPORT win the radio rights for England's winter tour to Pakistan. Kelvin told me he wanted live cricket rights and asked how we would go about it. I said you need to get to the right people and I had friends in Pakistan. It took me two phone calls to get to the head of Pakistan cricket, Salim Altaf – nicknamed Bobby. I had batted against him in Test matches at Lord's and Headingley in 1971 and told him the deal on offer. The BBC, not used to anyone else bidding, normally paid under £100,000 for the radio broadcast rights. I said that talkSPORT would give them a lot more, but we were not messing about or getting into a bidding war, so I gave them a couple of days and they came back and said fine. Nobody said a word, the BBC knew nothing about it. When they went for the rights, they found out they had already been sold and went doolally.

I did the same for the Sri Lanka tour that winter. This, in a small way, was how rights deals were starting to make money for cricket. When central contracts started in 2000, the PCA pushed for their members to receive a share and it was not long before they were taking home 11 per cent of the ECB's income. It is nonsense to put that all down to Packer. There is an argument to say he was the first one to put a value on cricket rights, but it took many years before that improved players' wages and by the time it did, Kerry Packer was dead.

So what does the game owe Packer now? Day/night cricket, and even then he pinched the idea off baseball in the United States and it worked only because in the warmer countries floodlit cricket is wonderful. His legacy? White balls, black sightscreens, coloured clothing and helmets. That is it. It was an awful lot of pain to endure for the birth of floodlight cricket, but unfortunately that does not fit the story for those who these days want to cast Tony as a hero and Packer as a saviour of the game.

And what about Tony? He had everything I ever dreamed of: he was captain of England, the pinnacle of English cricket, but he lost it all. Having led England on a highly successful tour of India where his leadership skills were praised by the players and media, he was absolutely on top of the mountain in his chosen sport and could have been England captain for years. His earning capacity, if not brilliant, was good and certainly better than any other cricketer at the time.

Why did he do it? It is a question that bothers me now and I still can't understand why he chose to jeopardise his job as England captain. Lots of theories were thrown around at the time, including the thought that Greig did not care about the

England captaincy because he was South African. In *The Times* John Woodcock wrote: 'What has to be remembered is that Greig is English not by birth or upbringing but only by adoption which is not the same thing as being English through and through.'

Answering that criticism, Tony always said: 'When I put on the Three Lions for England, I played and gave everything.' He would also mention his father fighting in the war and putting his life on the line for this country. Nobody questions his father's loyalty to England, or what he did while serving in the Royal Air Force during World War Two. Sandy Greig was a squadron leader by the age of 21 and flew 54 missions over Germany for Bomber Command, earning the Distinguished Service Order and Distinguished Flying Cross.

But Tony always missed the point: that was what his father did and not him. Just because his father fought heroically in the war, it should not have given Tony a free pass to play for England when he had not grown up here. After his father was shot down in the war, he went to South Africa to train pilots and met Tony's South African mother. Tony grew up in South Africa and went to Queens College, Queenstown and did not come to England until the summer of 1966, aged 19, when he had a trial at Sussex and then played in their second team. He came to England to use that passport of convenience inherited from his father because he knew the prospects were better here.

I have never agreed with cricketers moving to England and using this country as a ticket to international cricket. I have no problem with where people are born; babies have no choice because their parents could be working abroad. Men like Colin

Cowdrey, Andrew Strauss, Ted Dexter and Nasser Hussain were born overseas, but lived in England for most of their formative years. But there have been plenty of others for whom that was not the case.

My point here is not personal. Tony's sister Sally became a very good friend of mine and still is today, and she plays golf with my wife and me. When, in 1989, Tony's father had a heart operation which meant he could not fly back home to South Africa for many months, and Sally would ring up and say: 'Daddy's dying to talk cricket. Can I drop him off for a few hours?' She would deposit him in Woolley and he would stay all morning to while away the time.

I believe if you want to play for England at cricket, you should have attended school here and spent a long period of time in this country before you play for our national team. It is not how good you are, or how likeable you are, and it has nothing to do with race, colour or creed. I was brought up wanting to play for Yorkshire and England, and if my place had been blocked by somebody who spent 19 years in another country and suddenly took my place I would have been furious.

In 2012, the ECB recognised the problem and decided that England would go beyond the ICC regulations and impose a seven-year residency for English qualification, having decided the previous qualifying period of four years was too short. The ECB have taken the right step by making it seven years, but I would have gone further and made it ten.

Look at the recent England team. Jonathan Trott played for South Africa Under-19s but has played 49 Tests for England. How can that be right? I know he has a British father and an English wife, but that is irrelevant to me. If he thought he could have played international cricket for South Africa, would he have stayed there?

Kevin Pietersen is a similar case. I am guessing they come for the money and maybe a safer way of life, it's certainly not the climate. I love his batting and think he is a fantastic player, but he should be playing for South Africa. He made a clear-cut, ruthless decision to follow his career in England. He started out in South Africa and then moved to England because he thought he would get a county contract and his earnings capacity would be bigger. Eventually, he hoped it would lead to playing for England, which opens up many commercial opportunities these days.

I also don't agree with cricketers from Ireland playing for England. It is not personal. Eoin Morgan, for example, is a gifted one-day batsman blessed with a magical eye and wonderful hands. But the question is: are you British for convenience sake or are you really British?

This question continued to plague Tony for the rest of his life, especially when it was brought up in relation to the Packer affair. However, he brought a lot of the criticism on himself, as it was his choice to sign with Packer. Where he has been unfairly treated is that his cricket talent has been forgotten down the years, because people focus on Packer. It is a shame because he was an excellent player. As an all-rounder, he was more of a batsman who bowled and he was a terrific catcher, probably the best tall slip catcher I have ever seen.

His Test batting average was over 40, and his swing and seam bowling brought him 141 wickets at 32.20 which was pretty good. He was a clever cricketer, too. When he went to the West Indies in 1974, he could not get any swing or seam going in those conditions. He was walloped in the first two Tests, taking only three wickets for 166 runs. Then Raymond Illingworth, who was on the tour as a writer because they had given the captaincy to Mike Denness, suggested to Greigy: 'You have got big hands. Why don't you bowl more off-cutters, as they have got a lot of left-handers.' Roy Fredericks, Alvin Kallicharran, Garfield Sobers and Clive Lloyd were all left-handers who batted in the top six. Greigy took Raymond's advice and bowled off-cutters, taking six for 164 in the third Test on a good pitch in Barbados, and made 148 with the bat as well.

We then went to Trinidad for the final Test and he bowled them out twice with eight for 86 in the first innings and five for 70 in the second. Greigy had made it tough for them, by bowling with a high action, getting plenty of bounce and cutting the ball away from the left-handers. He was even awkward for right-handers, because in those days the Port of Spain pitch always turned. I made 99 and 112 and we won the game from nowhere.

After peace was brokered over the Packer affair, I had little contact with Tony for more than ten years, apart from in 1980 when he was working for Channel 9 in Australia and interviewed me as an England player after winning two man of the match awards against Australia. The next time I met up with him was on England's tour to the West Indies in 1990. Mark McCormack's company Trans World International (TWI) had bought the TV rights and sold them to the fledgling satellite company Sky. Tony was freelancing and fronted the whole show for TWI. I joined the commentary team of Tony Cozier, Michael Holding and Tony Lewis. Greigy had been commentating for nine years and I was the new boy.

We immediately gelled and received wonderful compliments when we were on air together. It was Tony who suggested to TWI that I should do the pitch reports, because he said that I read pitches better than anyone else. Ian Wooldridge wrote a smashing piece in the *Daily Mail* about how much he enjoyed us together and called it the Greigy and Fiery Show. We spent three months together and it was as if the whole Packer episode had never happened. We played golf together on days off, had dinners together and I loved it. It was a fun time.

Tony was also the person who got me to start wearing a hat. He'd started to wear one himself while working for Channel Nine TV in Australia, because he often had to stand out in the middle in the glaring sun while waiting for the producer to give the go-ahead to start his pitch reports. Sometimes there can be hiccups and you wait for ages to start.

That West Indies series was so successful for Sky that the next summer they bought the 40-over Sunday League competition in England, and signed up Tony and me to commentate, and he came over to organise and host the coverage. After that I worked with him on numerous occasions in India, Sri Lanka, Bangladesh, Sharjah and England. During our spells in commentary boxes around the world, I often teased him with the question: 'Who are you supporting today, Australia, South Africa or England?' Our colleagues in the commentary box invariably shouted: 'Whoever is winning.' He would just give that big smile and his infectious chuckle.

We never once mentioned the Packer period, I think we both felt it was too painful an issue and we did not want to resurrect it. We got on so well in later life that I don't think either of us wanted to spoil it. We were able to move on. As the years went by, I think he laid the Packer period to rest and made up with most people. I don't think he changed his view, and why should he? Packer had been very loyal and good to him.

However, it took the England authorities nearly 20 years to make him an honorary life member of MCC in 1998. This distinction is normally granted to all England captains after they retire. In Greigy's case, it had needed a period of cooling off and a change of regime at the top of English cricket. I don't believe it should have taken so long and I wrote to him at the time to say: 'Making you wait that long is wrong and unfair. Your record with England will stand any scrutiny from friends or enemies. It is an excellent one – something you can rightly be proud of.'

Tony Greig was no saint, but neither am I. He caused a lot of pain with his involvement in Packer cricket, but he could also be engaging, warm, and loved chatting about cricket over dinner with a glass of wine in his hand. We got on well as teammates, but for a decade our friendship was a victim of the Packer affair. We got over it, but that does not mean I should try to change history just because he was my friend.

CHAPTER 7

CLOUGHIE MY FRIEND

When I look back and think about all the people I have met during my life, there is one man who has left a lasting impression and, if circumstances had been different, could have had a huge impact on my cricket career: Brian Clough. I know he was a football man, the greatest manager of them all, but he loved his cricket too and we were very close friends for many years.

It always intrigues me when I hear successful people say they have never made mistakes during their lives, they must be joking or lying. As we get older, most of us learn from our experiences and become more mature and better people. At times in life we need someone to lean on, to offer advice and point out our mistakes; Brian did that for me when he could, but I just wish he had been around all the time.

Nowadays, the England cricket team have coaches for every

specific role. Every time I look, there is a new face, and I wonder what they can have been brought in to do. When I played we had no one to support us in the way that modern teams do. I had a bat, some gloves and some pads – that was it. There was nobody to manage or help us. When I was captain of Yorkshire, I was not even allowed to have Ted Lester, the team scorer, help me out. He travelled with us all the time and I wanted him as team manager, but it was blocked by the Yorkshire committee. This was a guy I revered, he played for eight years with great players like Len Hutton and a young Fred Trueman in his pomp, but the committee said no. Do it your bloody self was the message. It was penny-pinching and left me isolated, with so many other things to distract me from my main aim of leading the side to success. Brian would have seen that. He would have had the ability to spot I needed help.

I first met Brian when he was a centre forward playing for Sunderland and I was a young cricketer for Yorkshire. In those days, we used to play a lot in Scarborough during the high summer. Remember that back then working people very rarely went abroad for their holidays, instead many of them went to cricket festivals at places like Scarborough, Bridlington, Blackpool and Skegness. Games at those seaside venues were big occasions; the holidaymakers would go to the beach in the morning and, when the tide came in, the Scarborough cricket ground would fill up. Obviously there were die-hard fans there from the start of play who had just come over for the cricket, but mainly it was people having their only holiday of the year.

Cloughie would train in the morning with Sunderland and then travel down to Scarborough to watch the last two sessions of play. He would sit in the players' area, watching avidly. It was not a social outing for him; he would sit there and really watch and study the cricket. I can picture it now; it was one of those high summer days when I met him, sat in the Scarborough pavilion. I was introduced to him by Brian Close and in time Cloughie would become a lifelong friend. Years later, when Yorkshire played at Worksop near Nottingham, he would come to the ground, sit in a chair with a pint of beer and watch every ball with a couple of mates. He was not interested in going to the committee room, he just loved watching cricket and understood the nuances of the game.

When he retired from playing and became a football manager, I would travel to watch his teams at Derby County and Nottingham Forest, and he, in return, would come to see me bat. When I went to football matches at Derby or Forest, he would organise my director's box seat, a nice lunch before the match, sometimes in the same hotel as the players. After the match I would be invited into his office. Many a time I would be there chatting and the opposition manager would come in and have a drink before their team bus left. They usually came to pay their respects, because Forest had won and sometimes Brian's team had enjoyed a great result midweek in the European Cup.

As soon as Brian had finished work, he would say 'right let's go' and I would follow him in my car to his house in Derby. He always cooked dinner for me. I sat in the lounge talking to his wife, Barbara, and he would keep popping in from the kitchen where he would be cooking a steak. We would talk for a long time. I would want to talk football and he always wanted to talk cricket. If I wanted to take the mickey out of him, I would wait until I was talking to Barbara over dinner and would ask her: 'Who is your favourite player?'

She would reply Archie Gemmill and then go on to say: 'And I don't know why Brian sold him?' It was funny to get her started on the subject, but he would just sit back and roll his eyes because he knew what was coming.

I remember he had this rocking chair in his lounge at his house in Derby with the fire on the right-hand side and the television in the corner. Many team formations, transfers and European Cup campaigns were plotted in that rocking chair by the fire.

People thought he used to shoot from the hip, was full of himself and that's why he was called Ol' Big Head. They were wrong. He studied people and that was his great strength. When he made his outrageous comments, he usually did it for a reason, mostly to protect his players. He once said to me: 'They are paid to play, and in the end I do not have to go out and score a goal.' He was very clever as he took the pressure off them by making himself the focal point.

One of his innovations was that he realised very early on that the football season was a long slog, and the players and manager would see each other virtually every day for ten months. So he introduced breaks or holidays for the players and staff when he would send the team off to Spain, but he did not go with them. He stayed away because he thought they had seen enough of each other. Then sometimes unannounced he would disappear; the players would be expecting him at training but they would not see him all week, as he had gone on holiday and it kept everyone on their toes. There is a need to keep the players and manager fresh in sport, something cricketers are fully aware of after months on tour together.

The club would sometimes block some of his more ambitious holiday plans. In 1972, there was a Boxing Day match at Derby against Manchester United which County won 3–1, and afterwards there was a party for the players and their wives and he invited me along. He said he wanted to take some time off to 'watch Muhammad Ali fight, Frank Sinatra sing and Geoffrey play cricket'.

He did manage to fly to America in 1973–74 to see Ali fight Joe Frazier, but I'm not sure he saw Sinatra sing. He was planning to end the trip by flying to the West Indies to watch me play for England while we were on tour in the Caribbean, but he never made it that far, as he had to come back to work in the end.

I remember when I was going through my three-year break from playing for England, Brian would ask me if the then chairman of selectors, Alec Bedser, had been in touch. I explained Alec would phone me up once a summer, but Brian would keep pushing: 'Has he been to see you in person?' He could not understand why he had not travelled to see me. He said: 'If I were the chairman, I would come to your house and stay there and talk to you until I got you to agree to play for England. You are the best batsman, England are better with you playing. That would be my job: to get you batting for England at your best.' When you say it like that, the art of player management seems so simple, whatever the sport.

Would it have worked if Alec had come to see me? I don't know. Alec was a lovely man, but he did not have the Cloughie type of personality to carry it off, even if the idea had entered his head in the first place. Alec thought it wasn't his job to try to persuade or encourage any player to play for England. He probably felt once he had made his one obligatory phone call a year then that was all that was required of him and his selection committee. You could not say he was wrong, but he did not have the imagination to think differently.

Brian's gift was to understand people. There are lots of stories about him, but the best one for giving an insight into how he understood people was when Nottingham Forest played Liverpool in the first round of the European Cup in 1978.

Forest were the champions of England and Liverpool the European Cup holders. Forest won the first leg at the City Ground 2–0, but Brian sensed his players were terrified of playing Liverpool at Anfield in the second leg. On the way to the match, Brian could feel the tension so he stopped the bus at the next pub, brought on some beers and told the lads to have a drink, and those that smoked to get their cigarettes out and have a fag. They then had a sing-song on the way to the match, which was the biggest game of their careers at that point. When they arrived, they were not afraid of anything. To have the intuition to sense they were too tense to play, and then the courage to rectify that by letting them have a drink, knowing that if they lost he would be crucified by the press, was brave as well as inspired. I know times have changed, but can you imagine any manager doing that these days? No chance.

Forest drew the second leg 0–0, went through to the next round and eventually won the European Cup that season, beating Malmo 1–0 in the final, with Trevor Francis scoring the winning goal. They repeated the feat the following year, but if Brian had not shown that stroke of genius on the bus to Anfield many months before, then they might have lost that game and history would have been different.

I once had a more personal glimpse of his man-management skills. In June 1974, he came to watch me bat against Derbyshire in a championship match at Chesterfield. It was a beautiful day, I was in really good form but early on I pulled Alan Ward straight to the fielder at midwicket, Brian Bolus, and was out for four. I was beside myself with disappointment, and after a little while Brian came in to see me. I apologised to him and said I had 'ruined the day'. I will never forget what he said to me: 'Look, you see your colleagues outside. They are not sure if they will make a hundred now or ever again. You will get one, if not tomorrow then the week after. You will get plenty, because you are that good.'

I had just failed and he made me feel ten feet tall. That was his gift: he had a way of cutting to the quick. He saw the situation, understood it and turned it into a positive without making it seem small. It must have been unbelievable to play for him, as he gave players absolute belief in their abilities.

There were times when I was down and not playing well; most sportsmen have those moments. Only geniuses such as Donald Bradman, Bobby Jones, Pelé and Jack Nicklaus live on a constant high. Most of us are just talented with moments of insecurity, we need people like Brian Clough with the personality, knowledge and intuition to pick us up. It is not simply a question of saying a few words of reassurance, it is saying the right thing and knowing what to say and when to say it.

Brian's greatest skill was understanding people and putting round pegs in round holes. He did not tell players to improve on their weak points or negatives, he just wanted them to do the job he thought they were good at so he could put the jigsaw of the 11 players together.

I once asked him why he had picked Alan Hinton. He was the Derby County left-winger, who was a bit timid and did not tackle well. Remember, in those days it was a rough game. If you were a shy individual or a skilful winger, you got out of the way of the rough stuff and stayed on the wing. Hinton appeared a bit frightened of tackling, but Brian told me: 'Listen. I don't pay him to tackle; I pay him to pass the ball on to my centre forward's head and he is bloody good at that.' It stuck with me. It was Brian's job to find someone else to do the tackling, he saw what a player could do and asked him to play to his strengths.

I used to love going into his office to chat about football. His assistant Peter Taylor would be there as well; he was like a lovable cockney spiv, fast talking, funny and amusing. I remember when Brian bought David Nish, a midfielder from Leicester for £225,000, which was a lot of money in 1972, and played him at left-back. I couldn't understand why he had paid all that money for a midfielder and stuck him at left-back. Peter Taylor used to love those conversations. 'Here, sign him up as a coach, Brian,' he would say, taking the mickey. It is well documented he later fell out with Taylor, but Brian said to me: 'I loved Peter because he made me laugh every day I came into work.' He deeply regretted they fell out.

We sometimes even talked about possible signings. One day in his office in 1979, Brian said to me. 'I want a left-footed left-back.' He said he fancied Frankie Gray from Leeds, Eddie's brother. I didn't agree, and said I thought he was a winger and not a very good tackler. There was I telling one of the great managers how to do his job. Ludicrous really, but I could get away with it because he was my friend.

A few weeks later, I went off on tour with England. I came back months later and went to one of the end-of-season matches at Forest. Afterwards we went back to his house as usual. He was cooking me dinner, popping in to the sitting room chatting away with Barbara and me, and eventually he said: 'Oh, by the way, that left full-back I bought – our supporters voted him player of the year.' There was of course no 'by the way'; he had been waiting to tell me he knew more about football than me.

Like most successful men Brian was flawed, he was not perfect. There was talk he took backhanders, but I have no knowledge of that. However, the one injustice he has suffered is the suggestion that when he managed Leeds in 1974 he was an alcoholic. In *The Damned United*, author David Peace writes about his alcoholism during that period of his life, but it was not correct and Barbara and the family were really hurt by that.

I was his friend and admirer, but I am not blind to the fact he did become an alcoholic at the end. The pressures got to him after so many years in the job, but that was later on, not in 1974. Peace was unfair and should be ashamed of putting that in his book, even if it was supposed to be a work of fiction. Many people do not realise it is fiction, and read it because they think it is a true story about Brian Clough. Mud sticks and people out there believe Brian was on the booze when he was Leeds United manager. As a public figure, you have to live with the mistakes you make, but it really hurts you, and your family, when people write untruthful stories.

When he joined Leeds United in July 1974, I was one of the first people to see him. He was announced as the new manager on Wednesday 31 July. Yorkshire had played a three-day match at Lord's, which finished the day before, and I had netted at Headingley on the Wednesday morning and then drove to Elland Road to see him. I naively thought I would be able to pop in and have a chat, thinking there would be nobody about. When I arrived at Elland Road, there were press men and television crews everywhere. I went up to a window to talk to a secretary who was taking messages for Brian. I was in a queue of journalists hoping for interviews and she was writing all the messages down. I asked if I could see him and was told to wait. She had written all the names of the people wanting to see him and took a long list to his office. Eventually, she came back and told all the television and media men that he was with the chairman and too busy, but added: 'Mr Boycott, can you wait? He will come and get you.'

I went into his office and sat down with him for half an hour, that is how close we were. He had just arrived, taken training for the first time and seen the chairman. He had a piece of paper in front of him and he had already worked out the average age of the team, and some of the playing staff were getting old. Johnny Giles was nearly 34, Billy Bremner was approaching 32 and Norman Hunter was coming up to 31, while Terry Cooper was 30 and eventually moved on that year. He knew he needed an injection of youth without breaking up the team, and he had no sense of foreboding about the job; he was positive and confident about his own ability. When he was asked by one of the Leeds players: 'What can you do for us that we have not done already?' he answered: 'Do the same again and do it better.' He oozed ambition and drive.

Later on, he never said a lot about his time at Leeds United.

It was such a painful experience that he did not want to be reminded about it, but occasionally he would let slip the odd remark. I know he felt that behind his back Johnny Giles had played a part in his downfall. When Don Revie left, he had recommended Johnny to the Leeds United board as his successor. I'm guessing being overlooked can't have gone down very well with Johnny, and I know the feeling well because when Mike Denness got the England captaincy over me I was not best pleased. So he definitely started with a sceptical and wary team.

Another factor was not having Peter Taylor as his assistant to watch his back did not help. In their partnership, it was always Peter who stayed with the players and he could smell trouble or problems looming before they got out of hand. Brian felt that without Peter around, the players were left with more opportunities to plot. Peter was the fast talker, a lovable rogue, quick-witted with great one-liners and funny asides that kept the players on their toes and laughing. At stressful times he could lessen the tension and break the ice.

Brian believed that sometimes when he walked into the Leeds dressing room, the conversation suddenly stopped in its tracks, and he had a feeling the players had been talking about him and not in a nice way. When there is an atmosphere in the room you can sense it, we have all had that experience. What you have to remember is this successful Leeds United team had adored the previous manager, Don Revie, and in the past Brian had been openly critical of aspects of their play, such as fouling, having a poor disciplinary record, haranguing referees over decisions. One player in particular, Peter Lorimer, was an example of all he deplored. He was a very talented footballer, but Brian believed that far too often he fell down too easily to persuade referees into giving penalties.

Brian actually felt Revie had assembled a talented bunch of players who didn't need to do those things, as they were good enough without the gamesmanship, but his previous comments had caused resentment and anger. Maybe deep down some of the staff felt if they got on with this new guy, they were in some way being disloyal to their former manager. The club should have been aware Brian was going into a hostile environment, because everyone knew his views on Revie. Typical of the man, he had such self-belief in his own ability that he thought he could turn it around. He exuded confidence and thought managing the Division One champions was where his talent should be seen. He had spent six months in relative obscurity at Brighton, working with players who were not very good, and so this was an opportunity he could not turn down.

While he was working at Brighton, Barbara and the kids had stayed in Derby, which he had found very difficult. He liked being at home, he hated travelling from Derby to Brighton and here was a chance to be in the limelight again closer to home. He loved being on stage when it was football, but then when it was not football he wanted a quiet home life.

Leeds were playing in the European Cup as well. He had won the First Division at Derby and had a taste of European football with them, so it was natural he wanted another go. He had bought and sold players at Derby to make a successful team; he had trained and managed them well. He knew he could do it again. His self-belief was so strong, he believed that if the Leeds United directors had the gall to pick him as their manager, then he had the balls to take it on.

They sacked him after 44 days on 12 September 1974. The first thing he did was get the best solicitor he could find to negotiate his pay-off, his deal included a new Mercedes car and £98,000, which was a lot of money then, and enabled him to pay off the mortgage on his house. Immediately after Brian was sacked, he appeared on a television programme with Don Revie, by now the England manager. Revie gleefully tried to bait Brian by asking how he thought he could improve on the Leeds team that had lost only twice in a season. Typical of my friend, quick as a wink he answered: 'I could have gone through the season without losing one match.' That was the man summed up.

I once asked if he would be interested in managing my team, Manchester United, this was just before Alex Ferguson got the manager's job in 1986. I had started following Manchester United in 1962 after they signed Denis Law. He had been my favourite player ever since I first saw him play as a scrawny kid at Huddersfield Town, who were in the First Division and Bill Shankly was the manager. I used to go to the home games with my uncle Jack, and would ride in the sidecar of his motorbike to Leeds Road, Huddersfield's ground in those days. Denis was the same age as me and at 16 was the least likely footballer you have ever seen in your life. He had his collar up and sleeves down over his hands as if he was freezing to death. It was a rough game then, with a heavy ball, horrible pitches and hard tackling. He looked as though he didn't want to be there, until the ball came and then suddenly he came alive – he was like lightning.

I followed his career, and when he joined United from Torino I started going to Old Trafford. I used to stand on the terraces every fortnight in lot number 13 in what is now the Sir Alex

Ferguson Stand. I would get there early so I could stand right on the halfway line. I queued up with my sandwiches and flask of coffee for two hours before kick off, just to watch Denis and in doing so I fell in love with Bobby Charlton and Manchester United.

Anyway, when I asked Brian, he said he would have crawled up the motorway on his hands and knees to manage United, because he thought they were the biggest club in the country. Here was the most successful manager in England, winning the title with Derby and Nottingham Forest and two European Cups, but he was never offered the Manchester United job. In between Matt Busby retiring and Alex Ferguson taking over, Manchester United had five different managers but throughout that dismal period the best manager in England, Brian Clough, was never approached to take over the biggest club in the country. Extraordinary.

I asked him what he would have done if he had been appointed Manchester United manager. He said he would take all the players and staff around the trophy room, show them the cups and then close the cabinets up for good. 'We have to make our own medals and trophies now.' He was not showing disrespect to Matt Busby's legacy, he just knew the club could not live on memories.

It is what I told Yorkshire players in 2012 when I became the club's president. I told them the club has a great history but to forget about that. I said we want to win the championship in our 150th year in 2013, but you can't do that unless first you get out of the Second Division in 2012, which they did. I told them they had to make their own history. I was trying to use what I learned from Brian Clough: keep the message simple.

Brian knew how to handle the players. Sport is full of young, healthy, talented, cocky and confident kids, and you need to be strong to keep them in line because in their environment they are the heroes and can easily get too big for their boots. He gave them a structure. Discipline and time-keeping were paramount, they got fined if they were late. No swearing or arguing with referees or linesmen was allowed; he was the gaffer, he made it very clear he ran the club, full stop. They all knew if they stepped out of line too often he would not pick them.

His whole ethos about football was: don't complicate it. If you select the right players, if you train them the right way, manage them well, then they will be fine out on the park. He never had long tactical talks. Once at training he saw Kevin Hector, his centre forward, taking corner kicks. He said: 'What are you doing, young man? I pay you to get goals as my centre forward and you will not do that taking corner kicks. Now get in the penalty area.'

When you put it like that, you wonder why others were not as successful. The fact was, anyone could say something like that, but it was his knowledge and character that carried it off and made him special.

I remember a little Scottish centre forward he had at Nottingham Forest called Ian Wallace. At one stage, he had not scored a goal for weeks. Brian once told me that every Friday Wallace used to take Barbara some duck eggs, because Brian liked them for his breakfast. Peter Taylor said to Wallace, with Cloughie in earshot: 'We need a goal, I don't care if it is off the back of your head or the back of your arse, but we need a goal and those duck eggs won't save you unless you get one.'

Together Brian and Peter were magical. They spoke

common sense and got to the heart of the matter, but also made you laugh as well. Brian once explained football to me like this: 'You get the ball, play it on the floor, not in the sky, then you pass it to someone with the same coloured shirt, you play in their half more than in your own, and you put the ball in their net more than they put it in yours.' It sounded so easy, but we all know in reality it is not that simple and is bloody complicated, just like batting. Great people can break down sport into its component parts, otherwise you become so wrapped up in technique that you forget the real object is to hit or kick the ball.

When I coach cricket, I sometimes look at a player in the nets and think I could tell him ten things to work on, but if I do it will overload his brain and he will not be able to hit the ball. The clever thing is to choose a couple of things and pick him up as a person. That is what Clough did; as so often with great leadership, he had an instinctive gift. Michael Vaughan was a natural leader, he was born to it. Brian Clough was not coached to be a manager, it was natural. If people go to a cricket academy and learn strategies there, they will all come out like clones, thinking the same way. What you find in people like Brian and Michael is originality.

Brian could pick you up, but he could put you down as well. I saw his team win 5–0 once, and the players were full of joy in the dressing room, but he put his head around the dressing room door and said 'you should have got nine' and left them. He didn't want them getting too carried away.

Once they were losing badly at half time and all the players thought they would get a telling off. He did not appear in the dressing room at all, but just before they resumed the second half he popped his head around the door and said: 'My fault, I picked the wrong team.' That gave them something to think about and they went on to win the match.

Many people make excuses and blame others. He did not do that. Brian bought Gary Megson from Sheffield United for £176,000 in April 1974. There was a summer break and then pre-season training, but Gary never played a match for Brian. He was sold to Newcastle in September 1974 for £132,000. It seemed very odd, as Gary was a hard-working midfielder. When I asked Brian what happened he said: 'When you make a mistake, the best remedy is always to admit it as quickly as possible – and get rid.' He did not blame anyone else, but took responsibility for the mistake. He did add it was better for the boy to be playing football rather than being stuck in the reserves.

There was also a very generous side to Brian which I saw on several occasions. In 1980, when I moved to my house in Woolley, he rang me one day and said he was on his way over with a mate. He pulled up in his car with a trailer attached to the back. In it were eight gorgeous dwarf conifers and that mate turned out to be his gardener. While we had coffee in the lounge, Brian's gardener planted the trees. They were Brian's housewarming gift to me. Many people only knew of Brian's outspoken, abrasive side, but that was not the real man. When Nottingham Forest won the European Cup in 1979, he rang me and said he was popping over. He brought me a cut-glass replica of the European Cup they had just won.

Brian and I had similar backgrounds. We both came from poor mining areas, he in the Northeast and me in West Yorkshire. With not a lot of money coming in when we were kids, we couldn't afford to play anything other than football and cricket. Tennis and golf were middle-class sports and you had to have a lot of brass to join a club or buy the equipment. We had a football or cricket bat and ball and played in the streets with our mates. Perhaps it is one reason why we bonded.

Immediately after I scored my 100th hundred, in an Ashes Test match at Headingley in 1977, I telephoned two people; one was Michael Parkinson, the other was Brian. When I rang Brian's home, Barbara said he should have gone to a committee meeting that afternoon. In those days, Nottingham Forest was run by a committee, but she had to phone the club and tell them he was not moving because 'my mate is batting'. He sat and watched the whole lot on television and missed the meeting.

He loved a chance to play cricket, and one of his most enjoyable moments was when he got me out in a Lord's Taverners match at Lord's in 1975. The match was a special fixture in those days and would feature a mix of proper cricketers and celebrities. I played alongside Denis Compton, Ken Barrington, Tony Lewis and Richie Benaud. I remember hitting the first three balls of the match, bowled by Ted Dexter, for four. I had made over 50 when Brian came on to bowl, I smacked a couple of his off-spinners for boundaries but then chipped one back and he had me caught and bowled for 68. He was over the moon. He knew I had done it on purpose, but he was thrilled to bits. It was a lovely moment.

I don't know anybody who worked with Brian that did not have their lives changed by him in some way, most of them for the better. His former players talk about a strong-minded, brilliant manager. He must have done something right if they all say that.

In the end, the pressure of management was too much. I knew something was wrong in October 1992 when I went to see him in his last season at Forest. I watched his side play a dull 0–0 draw with Sheffield United. At the time, everyone was saying Forest were too good to be relegated because they always played lovely football, but it was rubbish; they were a shadow of Brian's attractive teams of the past. I saw him in his office after the game and he looked terrible. His nose and face were red and blotchy due to the alcohol; he was lifeless and not the Brian Clough I knew. I came away knowing they would be relegated, as he was not in any fit state to manage a team. Brian had thrived on energy and vitality and had not been afraid to make decisions. Now the force had gone out of him, it was like waiting for the guillotine. The alcohol made him inactive, he had lost the drive to go and buy players. I suppose it is what alcohol does to you in the end.

I saw him a few times after he retired, he loved growing sweet peas and spending time in his garden, but football had left a hole. He was not well, but kept it very private within the family.

In the summer of 2003, I was recovering from my tongue cancer and wanted to see Brian, so I contacted Barbara. Talking to Barbara I could tell he was poorly and I needed to see him. In January that year, Brian had undergone a liver transplant and Barbara wanted to get him out of the house, so his daughter Elizabeth agreed to drive them both up to my home for lunch. I was going overseas to commentate in early September and Barbara had confidentially kept me informed of his health and treatments he was having at the time. It was a lovely sunny day when they came to Woolley, and we sat in our conservatory chatting away. When I asked Barbara if she would like a drink, Brian piped up: 'I'd like a glass of white wine.'

During lunch he emptied his glass and asked Rachael for another. Rachael saw the look of disapproval, or what could have been disappointment and dismay, on the faces of Barbara and Elizabeth. But he was not the sort of man to confront even as ill as he was then, so Rachael said no problem, took his glass to the kitchen, filled it a quarter of the way up with chardonnay and topped it up with water. He took one mouthful and the sly old fox knew exactly what she had done and why. He just looked her in the eye with that naughty smile of his and nodded, but he never said a word.

Some weeks later, while I was still in Singapore commentating for ESPN, Rachael was at home when the phone rang very late at night. It was Nigel wanting to speak to me to let me know his dad had died and the family did not want me to learn about it in the media.

Nigel rang Rachael a few days later, asking when I would be back home in England, because Barbara and the family wanted me to speak at his memorial service. I was still doing studio work for ESPN in Singapore on the India v Australia Test matches, but I am so pleased that the family thought enough of me to hold the service when I could be available, and I thought so much of him that I suggested I would fly back for a few days. I arrived home on 19 October and the memorial service was held at Derby County's ground, Pride Park, on Thursday 21 October 2004, my birthday. It rained cats and dogs, a miserable evening, but 14,000 people came to pay their respects and I was one of the two speakers, along with Martin O'Neill.

It was sad, the end always is, but life is not about dying, it is about what you achieve while you are alive. He left lots of wonderful memories, his teams played fairly and he won trophies. He was larger than life, an interesting man and exceptionally talented both as a player and manager. Now when I think about Brian, I see him at Derby when he was so boyish, young and full of energy, he was like a whirlwind. I wish he had been my manager as well as a best friend, as he would have helped me make some better decisions because he just had a gift for seeing things so clearly.

As a man I loved Brian's company and admired his professional achievements. I wish he was still here.

CHAPTER 8

THE SLEDGING CURSE

There has been an enormous rise in the use of sledging in the modern game and sadly the authorities have failed to crack down on foul-mouthed players. It has reached the stage that sledging has become a way of life for today's cricketer, who sees it as being as normal as strapping on his pads or polishing the ball. If the ICC continue to ignore this rising bad behaviour and sledging, then eventually there will be a fight on the field and a player will clock someone. There is testosterone flowing during the pressure moments of a Test match, and players won't always take a backward step when they are confronted.

The Australians are the worst culprits. Baiting Englishmen has become a national sport for them. The players, public and media see us as fair game, but that should not be the case. Yes, the Ashes is a traditional sporting contest between two nations, but nothing more. It means a lot, but it is not about fighting each other. If I remember rightly, we fought two world wars side by side. We are friends and allies, but on England's last tour to Australia the players knew they were on enemy territory.

The tone was set by Michael Clarke and Darren Lehmann. The captain and coach of Australia have a lot to answer for, because they should set an example. Ask people in the armed forces. Guys at the top set the standards and you have to follow them. The discipline is there. It should be the same in sport. But Clarke resorted to foul-mouthed abuse as soon as the series started, and Lehmann set the ball rolling even before England set foot in Australia. It was all very distasteful.

The first Test at the Gabba marked a new low. Two Australian players, David Warner and George Bailey, behaved appallingly and Clarke was picked up on the stump microphone giving the public an insight into the kind of abusive language players throw at each other these days. Clarke purposely walked up from second slip and said to England's tailender, James Anderson, that Australia would 'break his fucking arm'. It was a horrible comment.

These players think they are being clever, hard men, but it is crude, offensive and dragging cricket through the dirt. As soon as a new player breaks into the team, he starts the foul-mouthed verbals from day one, as if he has to prove his toughness to the others.

Look at George Bailey. There he was on his Test debut at the Gabba giving Anderson, England's last man, a gob full of abuse from short leg as Australia closed in on a massive victory. Bailey was 31. The public, the selectors, and probably even he himself were not sure if he was good enough for Test cricket, but he obviously felt confident enough to lay into Anderson, one of the best bowlers in the world, because sledging is second nature to the modern player. I know Anderson dishes it out and is no saint. He is a fast bowler who gets stuck in to batsmen verbally, but there was no need for Bailey to abuse a No 11, who was already scared enough trying to work out how he would cope with the pace of Mitchell Johnson.

Instead of showing some proper leadership, Clarke threatened Anderson in the crudest manner possible after the England bowler had stuck up for himself and had a go back at Bailey. Clarke must have thought he was being a clever dick. I never heard him acting so nasty when Australia were being beaten by England in the previous three series. He was the most mild-mannered and likeable guy you could meet, but then I thought he changed once his team started winning. He should remember it is important to win with dignity. If the captain behaves that way, should we be surprised if his players follow suit?

We all know David Warner is not exactly the nicest person on the planet. A fine player, yes, but some of his behaviour, such as attempting to punch Joe Root in a Birmingham bar in 2013, has shown what he is capable of when riled. At the Gabba, he got in on the act in a public way by rubbishing Jonathan Trott in a press conference. He implied Jonathan Trott was scared against Johnson, saying he was 'pretty poor and pretty weak'. While he was not to know that Trott would be going home a few days later with a 'stress-related illness', it was disrespectful of him to make such comments to the media about a fellow professional. England were right to be very angry. What would the Australians have said if the England players had made comments in public about Warner's episode when he threw a punch at Joe Root?

I don't remember any of our guys saying anything in press conferences or interviews. They were told to keep quiet. They did not go public saying exactly what they thought of Warner. All hell would have broken loose if they had called him a 'talented scrubber'.

Warner is just a product of the system and his behaviour was part of a systematic attempt to unsettle England with abuse, and for that Darren Lehmann has to take a lot of the blame. I love Darren. He played at Yorkshire with distinction for a number of years and is probably the best overseas player we have ever had. He is a great guy, a tough competitor and lives for cricket, but he incited the Australian crowds to abuse Stuart Broad on England's tour to Australia and that was unacceptable.

It all stemmed back to the first Ashes Test in the summer of 2013 at Nottingham. Broad nicked a delivery from the left-arm spinner Ashton Agar, which ricocheted off Brad Haddin, the wicketkeeper, and was caught by Clarke at first slip. Broad stood his ground and was given not out by umpire Aleem Dar. He was on 37 and added a further 28 runs to his score.

At the time Lehmann kept his mouth shut and seemed to brush it off until the Ashes were lost. A few days before the final Test at The Oval, he gave a telephone interview with a laddish radio station in Melbourne and basically told the Australian public to abuse Broad in the return series a few weeks later. He called him a 'blatant cheat' and said he hoped the Australian fans would make his life such a misery that he 'cries and goes home'.

The Australian media picked up on it and before the first Test the *Brisbane Courier-Mail* wrote puerile articles on their front page calling on fans to abuse Broad. Lehmann started it and the boozed-up fans in the stands then felt emboldened to carry it on. Broad played all five Tests in Australia and at every ground the crowd sang 'Broady is a wanker'. That was just personal abuse after Lehmann had set a nation to get at one individual. I thought Darren was better than that; he did not have to stoop so low, and it was unnecessary as he later proved that his cricket brain was enough to beat England.

I admired Broad for the way he never complained and showed tremendous character. He is a strong, feisty bugger and I like that. You need to have aggression as a fast bowler, and he ended up being the best England cricketer on the tour despite the abuse. But he should not have had to put up with personal insults incited by the opposition coach. It was disrespectful, but I fear it will happen again and we will reach the point where a player could even be attacked by a fan.

Darren Lehmann was fined only 20 per cent of his match fee by the ICC for the Broad comments and there was no disciplinary measure forthcoming from his boss, James Sutherland, at Cricket Australia. Sutherland was also wishy-washy with Clarke. He should have told him the abuse of Anderson was not acceptable behaviour, especially for a captain, never mind a player, and publicly admonished him. But instead Clarke was fined only about £2,000 by the ICC, a piffling amount for today's multi-millionaire cricketers. Clarke is the highest paid sportsman in Australia, earning around A$2 million a year. Fining him £2,000 was pointless.

There was no immediate apology or sign of remorse, and to

top it all Channel 9 ended up apologising to Clarke for leaving the stump mic open, instead of turning it off, and getting the Australian captain in trouble. In my opinion Lehmann and Clarke should have been banned for the next two Ashes Tests and if it happened again, I would double the suspension to four matches. Hit them with a punishment that hurts. They have to learn there are boundaries you do not cross.

Six months later, Michael Clarke finally managed to say this: 'I regret the language I used, and I regret that I said it over the stump mic. The last thing I want is for boys and girls watching cricket to be going and playing club cricket and saying things like that to opposition players. I think it's unacceptable that the Australian cricket captain is setting that example. But I don't regret standing up for my team-mates one bit. I don't regret being extremely honest with James Anderson and telling him what Mitchell Johnson's plan was. I don't regret that – I just regret that everybody heard it and the language I used.' It was at best a half-hearted apology, because he seems to think what he said is all right, he's just sorry it was overheard! Maybe someone pointed out the possible repercussions.

If a mother hears her child swearing, she puts a stop to it and explains it is unacceptable behaviour; if she does not, the child, when hearing adults swear, thinks it is clever and does it again and again. Mothers know to put boundaries in place for the child's own good. They could teach our cricket administrators a thing or two about discipline. The ICC should call a summit of all the captains and coaches to tell them it has to stop or there will be suspensions. Sportsmen should not be allowed to get away with things on the field that are unacceptable in the real world.

My point about this trash talking is would these guys say it to someone in the pub? Would Clarke have threatened a taller lad like Anderson with breaking his arm? Of course not, because he would have got a bunch of fives and ended up flat on his back.

The modern cricketer buys into the myth that sledging has always been part of the game. Rubbish. There is nothing wrong with intimidation in a cricketing sense. Cricket is a test of people's courage and character. If a fast bowler hits a batsman in the ribs or on the head, fine. Bowlers like Joel Garner, Michael Holding, Colin Croft and Andy Roberts stared, and if looks could kill I would have been dead years ago. Short balls would whistle past my nose or over my head. I had no problem with that; it is part of the game for a fast bowler to rough up a batsman. If you can't take it, then pack away your bat and get a normal job; but I never heard those great West Indians swearing at a batsman.

The batsman has to be good enough, and brave enough, to cope with that. But I batted against some of the best and nastiest fast bowlers who have ever played the game and they did not sledge me. I was also part of a very good Yorkshire side captained by Brian Close, one of the hardest men to play cricket, but he did not resort to personal abuse.

Dennis Lillee and Jeff Thomson would turn the air blue during some overs, you would constantly hear the f-word, particularly when Thommo was bowling, but it was never aimed directly at the batsman, more a sign of his frustration. All he and Lillee ever did was try to knock my block off, but they never sledged me once. If I thick-edged a ball down to third man, they would swear but it was never personal abuse aimed directly at me. The best bowlers rely on their skill to get wickets not their tongue.

Brian Close would intimidate batsmen not by sniping from second slip but by fielding close in and staring at batsmen. One of our tactics at Yorkshire if we had spinners on and took a wicket was that we always made sure we were ready in our fielding positions when the next batsman came in to take guard. Fielders would be very close and bent down, looking at him from a yard away in order to put the pressure on (today players are too busy performing high fives and then congratulating each other in a huddle when they get a wicket). We saw body language as a tool for intimidation, not mouthing off. We were challenging the batsmen, implying we are ready to get you out. I don't remember us saying anything nasty.

Fred Trueman used to come out with funny remarks that would make people laugh when he was bowling. One of Fred's great sayings to a batsman if he nicked one through the slips was: 'Fuck me, you have more edges than a broken piss pot.' And we would all crack up.

One day a batsman kept playing and missing, and Fred said: 'Fuck me, hold the bat still and I will hit it.'

In its way it worked as a kind of mental put-down for the batsman, and in the heat of battle it made us all laugh. Fred would not have taken more wickets if he had resorted to personal abuse and, like Michael Clarke, said: 'I'm going to break your fucking arm.' Fred would have been tickled though to hear the hypocrisy of an Australian, Lehmann, criticising a batsman, Broad, for not walking.

I played 38 Test matches against Australia and I can say they never walk. In fact, Richie Benaud is on record as saying he was taught at school never to walk. Flick back through history and you will find plenty of examples. In 1946–47 at Brisbane during the first Test match after the war, Donald Bradman edged Bill Voce to Jack Ikin at second slip. He stood his ground and was given not out. He was on 28 at the time and went on to score 187.

There was talk before the Test that Bradman was past it and he would retire if he failed in Brisbane. He had been invalided out of the army during the war down to poor eyesight and there was a lot of speculation over his health. But he went on to finish his career with a mountain of runs. Wally Hammond, the England captain, said on the field after the Ikin incident: 'A fine fucking way to start a series.'

When I was playing, I always said you should wait for the umpire's decision. In the second Test of the 1965–66 Ashes series, I caught and bowled Doug Walters in Melbourne. He had scored a hundred on his debut in the first Test and then went on to score a century in the second innings of his second Test. It was very hot and the match was petering out in a draw, so Mike Smith, captain of England, bowled people like me to fill in and give the proper bowlers a rest. Doug Walters hit the ball straight back to me but stood, implying it had hit the ground first and was a bump ball. The umpire gave him not out and so he started his career with two hundreds in two matches.

W.G. Grace is reputed to be the most famous and most frequent non-walker of all time, so I say to people there is nothing new in not walking and Stuart Broad is not alone. The laws of the game say 'in the umpire's opinion', and the Broad incident was actually an example of terrible umpiring.

I could see clearly, sitting in the *Test Match Special* commentary box at Trent Bridge, that he edged it. It was a monumental howler by Aleem Dar. How could he not see the edge from 22 yards away? That decision probably cost Australia the Test match, as Broad's partnership with Ian Bell added another 59 runs and they lost the match by 14 runs. It should have been umpire Aleem Dar copping the criticism, not Broad. In some ways I admire Broad's gall to stand his ground. I would have been too embarrassed to stay, and most of us would have walked off because it was so obvious. The only reason we walk when we nick it to slip is because it is so clearly out. You would look stupid to stand there and wait for the umpire. We are deflated and walk off wanting to get back to the sanctuary of the dressing room.

At the time Broad was accused of breaking the Spirit of Cricket. Nonsense. The Spirit of Cricket is a nebulous theory that is spouted by people who believe everyone should do the decent thing and walk. It has not really been thought through. They may understand and love the game of cricket, but they are living in cloud cuckoo land if they think it will work. The Spirit of Cricket was thought up in the late 1990s by Colin Cowdrey and Ted Dexter and is widely promoted by the MCC, who have the good of the game at heart. But it should be used to regulate standards of behaviour by players not an issue such as walking.

The ICC has its own Code of Conduct, but perhaps it should be renamed the 'Spirit of Cricket' to punish players for disciplinary lapses such as sledging and general bad behaviour. Part of the problem with on-field behaviour is the umpires are too weak. I think I was lucky to play in an era of strong officials who had played the game. Now many of the ICC's Elite Panel (the umpires who stand in Test matches) have played very little international cricket. I always felt when I played county cricket, the ex-players were the better umpires because they knew all the dodges and scams. They too had tried it on when they played the game.

I am not saying good umpires need to have been great players, but at some point they will have shared a dressing room or played against top cricketers and that makes them less impressionable. These days I think umpires are dazzled by the big stars and in awe of them. That did not happen with umpires like Ken Palmer, Dickie Bird and Arthur Jepson, who had all played county cricket for years. With them if it was out, it was out. If a player had crossed the line or started getting lippy, it was dealt with regardless of who it was.

Bill Alley was also a strong umpire. When Ray Bright started verbally abusing me in 1977 as I was scoring my 100th hundred at Headingley, Bill nipped it in the bud. Bright thought he had me caught behind. Rubbish! I never touched it. I wouldn't have got out to Ray Bright, as he couldn't bowl. Dennis Lillee, yes; Ray Bright, no. Anyway, he was obviously upset with me, but Bill spotted what was going on and had strong words with him and Greg Chappell, the Australia captain, and put a stop to it. That was good umpiring. In fact I did not register a word of what Bright was saying, as I never let that type of thing affect my concentration. I used to chuckle to myself when people tried to sledge me: 'Carry on, when I am still here at tea you will need all your energy just to bowl at me.'

Administrators often say they leave it up to the umpires or 'we can only do anything if an umpire reports an incident to the match referee', but that's a cop out. At the Gabba when Bailey and Anderson were having the altercation, on seeing Clarke in the middle of an over walk up from slip, warning lights should have come on. Any umpire with any brains should have spotted what was going on and moved quickly towards the players to intervene before there was a chance of anything happening.

The reason I think this issue is so important and needs dealing with properly is that when incidents of sledging are seen on television by club cricketers and kids, they think it is okay for them to behave that way because the big stars get away with it without meaningful repercussions. As a result, umpires at club level now get more abuse than ever before. It overstepped the mark in the last two Ashes series and threatened to ruin one of the great sporting contests. I know that Australia won the Ashes back, but that does not justify their behaviour. I also recognise that England are no angels and if our players ever stoop so low, you will not hear me supporting them, I will be just as strong in my criticism. It would not be right and I hope our administrators would react better than the Australian board, but I'm not holding my breath.

CHAPTER 9

SAVING TEST CRICKET

I fear for the future of Test cricket more than any other aspect of the game. I would love it to survive for another 200 years, but it is being allowed to die by administrators too busy increasing their own power and too complacent to tackle the problems it faces.

What is going to happen over the next 30 to 50 years? The rich nations will get richer and the poor poorer. In early 2014, the International Cricket Council (ICC) was carved up by the big three – India, Australia and England. It was a power grab sugar-coated by statements saying it will benefit everybody. Rubbish. They scrapped plans for the World Test Championship and marginalised the smaller nations, while making all the right noises about supporting Test cricket. But do they really care?

The biggest bully of them all is the Board of Control for

Cricket in India (BCCI) and they have just made sure they are going to stay top dogs. Giles Clarke, the chairman of the ECB, was party to this coup along with Cricket Australia. As a result we will see more money from the ICC's television rights for the period of 2015–23 flow upwards to the big three, leaving the other countries even more powerless than they are now.

A tour by India is priceless to every other country. Look at South Africa. In January 2014, India pulled out of the Cape Town Test over a silly political spat involving Haroon Lorgat, the chief executive of the South African board. When he was chief executive of the ICC, he tried to curb India's power, so they took their revenge by pulling out of the New Year's Test in Cape Town. It cost the South African board £11 million in lost earnings. Other countries are terrified they might suffer the same consequences if they upset India. Should we blame India for being strong and flexing their muscles? Or do we blame other countries for being too weak?

In an ideal situation, cricket would have an independent body filled with people without a vested interest to run the world game, but that will never happen. Giles Clarke and his colleagues have seen to that. In 2011 Lord Woolf, the former Lord Chief Justice of England and Wales, was commissioned by the ICC to review its governance. He recommended the addition of independent directors to the ICC board to clamp down on decisions being taken with vested interests at heart, but his recommendations were ignored.

Cricket has now come full circle. In 1909 at Lord's, England, South Africa and Australia formed the Imperial Cricket Conference. In 1926, West Indies, New Zealand and India were made full members. Pakistan followed in 1952, Sri Lanka, Zimbabwe and Bangladesh joined later.

In 1965, the board became the International Cricket Conference and until 1993, when the board was renamed the International Cricket Council, England and Australia had two votes each. They had four out of eight votes before they started, so unless the other countries could split England and Australia they always had their way. It was disgraceful and other countries rightly felt it was a repugnant remnant of Britain's white colonial past. The balance of power began to tip India's way when voting was changed to one member one vote that year, and now they hold all the aces because they generate 80 per cent of the ICC's income from television rights. This has led to a greedy push for more influence.

From the last ICC television contract, India received $52 million out of a generated amount of $1.5 billion over eight years. Clearly they deserve more – nobody would argue with that – but not the 20 per cent share they will now have if the ICC sell their rights for their targeted $2.5 billion. Australia and England are hanging on to their coat-tails as an act of self-preservation.

How did they get away with it? Simple. The other countries do not have any leverage. If they had said they were going to refuse to play against England, India or Australia, they would have gone bankrupt within a couple of years. They were threatened and cajoled into signing up. Zaka Ashraf, the chairman of the Pakistan Cricket Board, abstained when they first tried to push through these changes. But when he went home he was sacked by his board. Why? Because India threw Pakistan a bone and hinted they might play them again in international cricket. It is what always happens when India wants Pakistan's vote. Pakistan know they will make a fortune from television rights if they play India, so they sacked Ashraf for trying to do the decent thing.

South Africa were brought into line with empty promises. Haroon Lorgat was not at the ICC meeting in Singapore when this decision was taken due to some dubious charges laid against him by the ICC, for allegedly playing a part in a state-ment which criticised the governing body over the row with India about the Newlands Test. He was later exonerated but missed the meeting, so the chairman of Cricket South Africa (CSA), Chris Nenzani, went in his place. The BCCI dropped hints they would shift some of the 2014 IPL to South Africa over security concerns in India, as the tournament coincided with the Indian general election. That would net CSA a lot of money and make up for the £11 million they lost over the Newlands Test. They voted for the changes, but the IPL began in the UAE instead.

The smaller nations were powerless, so they voted in favour of the new arrangements. After the power grab by the big three, Lord Woolf summed up the situation perfectly: 'I don't see how if we had this to consider we could see it as anything but a retrograde step. It is giving extraordinary powers to a small triumvirate of three people, and everybody else has got no power to say anything or do anything. To say a sport that has got aspirations to be a world-class sport internationally should not have an independent body at the top seems to me to be very surprising. It seems to be entirely motivated by money.'

Yes money, but also power. The men at the top have ensured they have the key jobs. N. Srinivasan, the chairman of the

BCCI, will be chairman of ICC in 2015. Wally Edwards, chairman of Cricket Australia, will be chairman of the ICC's new executive committee, while Giles Clarke has got the best job of all. He is a smart cookie and he has made sure he will remain chairman of the finance and commerce committee, the most powerful of the lot, negotiating all those lucrative television and radio rights deals. You can wrap it up in Christmas paper if you like, but it is a plain fact that where there is brass, there is power and that is what it is all about. It is not how I understand democracy to work. I know cricket has to make ends meet, but we want to keep the game alive everywhere, with all ten countries playing each other in a meritocracy.

It brings to mind *Animal Farm* by George Orwell. We have three pigs who have re-written the rules to say 'everyone is equal, but some are more equal than others'. The three pigs – England, Australia and India – are going to make squillions of dollars at the expense of the rest. It is a sad day for cricket.

People keep telling me it will be all right, that cricket has always faced problems and survived, but it is different now because for decades our administrators have been blind to the real issues because of the television money. The cash boards are raking in from broadcasting rights is growing all the time, the administrators love the television money, it is easy lolly and they do not have to do anything to sell the game. They just divide up a load of juicy fixtures, with England, India and Australia making sure they play each other the most often, and just wait for the television companies to start a bidding war for rights. But if television ever decides to desert the game and finds something else, then international cricket, and the counties, will be finished. And don't be fooled into thinking television will be loyal to cricket. It doesn't owe the game anything. If it finds tiddlywinks or poker attracts bigger audiences, then it will leave cricket tomorrow. It will not hang around.

But at the moment it is a seller's market. You have rival television stations scrapping over rights and boards flogging them for eye-watering amounts. As I've mentioned, the ICC are hoping to sell their next batch of rights for $2.5 billion. Even in England over the past 15 years, we have had the BBC, Channel 4, Channel 5 and Sky paying ever-increasing amounts to show cricket. Now BT Sport have entered the market and could be a serious rival to Sky for future international rights.

I know our board say the television money helps them invest in blind cricket, deaf cricket, women's cricket, junior cricket, inner-cities cricket and to shell out a few thousand here and there to clubs struggling to raise enough money to give the pavilion a lick of paint. That is philanthropic and very nice, but it does not help the game at the top level, because fewer people are coming through the gates to watch matches. Crowds are dwindling at Test matches around the world, apart from when England are in town. Anybody who fails to see that problem is sticking their head in the sand.

Ashes series are not the issue; grounds are full in England and Australia when these two countries play each other. They capture the imagination of the public and cricket lovers all over the world. It is an iconic series, bringing alive the history and tradition of the game. It is the dwindling interest in Test cricket when other nations are playing that worries me and should concern every cricket lover. If we carry on like we have been in recent years, with matches played in front of a decreasing number of spectators, we are going to get to a point when there is nobody in the grounds. It will take time, yes, but it will happen. A game cannot survive with empty stadiums no matter how big the television money; cricket needs bums on seats.

It is not a case of my being pessimistic; I recognise the fact that people pick up the paper to read about cricket or scan the web for scores and listen in their droves to the cricket on the radio. I understand there is as much interest as ever, but turning that into paying spectators is becoming harder and harder compared with years ago.

When I first toured South Africa in 1964–65, the Newlands Test was full, chock-a-block, you couldn't get a seat. It was the iconic place to be at New Year. These days, unless England are playing, you can walk up on any day to any Test match and pay at the gate. In Cape Town, except on weekends, they are lucky if it is even half full with maybe 10,000 people in the ground. There are empty seats galore. However, when England tour South Africa, it is like a home Test match for us because there are so many British tourists and Barmy Army people there on holiday.

It is the same situation when England play in Barbados: there are more English supporters on holiday with banners bragging about which football team they support than locals backing the West Indies. Without those England fans, you would be lucky to have a half-full stadium.

When I played in the Caribbean in 1968 and 1974, every ground was full; it was a huge event for the locals, who would turn up in their thousands to support the home team. The atmosphere was magical, just amazing. With Calypso bands, people blowing trumpets and conch shells, it was bloody noisy when you were batting, but you should have heard how many decibels the volume went up when they got a wicket. There were no televised matches in the West Indies until 1990, when satellite television started. Even then, the broadcasters were not allowed to show the match on the island where it was being played, as the signal was blocked out to encourage the local population to attend the match.

In India during the 1970s and even up to the 1980s, in Calcutta you could not get a seat during a Test. There would be 100,000 people inside at the game with a further 10,000 out-side, some with tickets still trying to get in. All hell would let loose, they would be so mad they would start throwing stones over the wall because they couldn't get in to watch the match. Now you can walk up and sit in any one of 80,000 bucket seats and watch whoever is playing.

Despite the declining attendances for Test matches, India makes more money out of cricket than any other country by a mile and produces 80 per cent of the income of world cricket. Why? Once again, television is the answer. Four or five televi-sion stations in India are queuing up for Test cricket and bid figures that are bigger than telephone numbers. In return for their money they want cricket matches – lots of them. As a con-sequence, because there is too much Test cricket, it is no longer considered a rare event. It is like if you miss the bus and there is another one along in ten minutes, you are not bothered. But if there is only one bus a day, you bloody well make sure you are at the bus stop early so as not to miss it. That is how Test cricket used to be.

The administrators don't seem to care; they just want to put on more matches, which brings in more TV money and keeps the broadcasters happy. Satellite television loves cricket. Why?

It is brilliant because it fills so many hours of airtime. You can have a one-hour show before play, six and a half hours of action, with long breaks for lunch and tea. It has stats and gizmos galore. They have Hawk-Eye, Snicko, and mobile cameras hovering in the air called the spider cam, stump cams and stump microphones and inane player interviews before, during and after play.

In addition, there are natural breaks at the end of every over to show adverts, which in India rake in huge amounts of money. Add in drinks breaks, batsmen getting out and it is perfect for advertisers. Which other sport gives TV that?

Television audiences are up, so the advertisers see it as a chance to flog their goods, meaning broadcasters can charge more for adverts. Everyone makes money, but sod the actual numbers at the ground.

Over-rates do not encourage spectators to come to the grounds either, because they never know what time the match is going to finish. There is too much dawdling around, time-consuming discussions between bowler and captain that take forever. We have endless player huddles in the middle of a game and an amazing amount of drinks interruptions. The slightest bit of drizzle or bad light and they are off.

Twenty years ago, I suggested we should bring in penalty runs to punish teams for slow over-rates. It should not be difficult to bowl 15 overs an hour minimum. I look back at England's tour of Australia in 1970–71, when we bowled eight-ball overs. In the drawn Tests at Brisbane, Perth, Melbourne and Adelaide, where we played out the full hours, we got through the equivalent of at least 100 six-ball overs *in a six-hour day*, the lowest being 494 overs in five days at Melbourne, the highest 505 in the match at Adelaide.

Both sides had fast bowlers: Garth McKenzie, Dennis Lillee and 'Froggie' Thomson for the Aussies and John Snow, Ken Shuttleworth, Bob Willis and Peter Lever for us. No one had a run-up as long as Lever and, as someone said at the time, 'I don't go as far as that for my holidays.' Plenty of batsmen got injured, the temperature was red-hot everywhere, we all got tired, there were drinks intervals and wickets tumbling, but we still got through the overs on time and without any of these stupid allowances.

To stop the dawdling, I believe we should penalise the bowling team 10 runs for every over they are short at the end of an innings or end of the day. That would mess them up good and proper, because it could cost the team a match. Hurt players where it matters, during the match they are trying to win, not afterwards with small fines.

But what did the ICC do? They brought in meaningless fines instead that do not work, because nowadays most of the players are wealthy young men. At the end of the game, the match referee can suspend captains for future Tests, but they hardly ever use this power, except to punish players from the smaller countries who will not make a fuss. All the match referees are ex-cricketers and they do not feel comfortable suspending players. A punishment after the event allows a captain and his players to get away with bowling their overs slowly and indulge in gamesmanship. It is a cheats' charter.

So what is the solution to this problem? In 2005, I delivered the Cowdrey Lecture at Lord's for the MCC. In it, I advocated four-day Tests of seven hours each day, with a guaranteed 15 overs an hour. That's 105 overs a day, 420 in a match. Currently, there are supposed to be 450 overs in a Test, based on 90 overs a day for five days. However, that's only if you are lucky, because on most occasions teams do not bowl their overs at the required rate and some overs are lost. A large per centage of games now finish inside the allotted time, with 75 per cent of Tests completed inside four days, the full 450 overs aren't needed. So I think we need to concertina the game to concentrate the action while losing none of the skills.

Thanks to modern bats, players score quicker now than ever before and you have more wins and losses, even though the over-rate is down to 13 an hour. Players get out because they are playing one-day strokes in Test cricket. They invent shots and take risks in one-day and Twenty20, and then transfer that to the longer format of the game. They score quicker but make more mistakes. It is wonderful, interesting cricket and a great product to watch, but could be wrapped up in four days if modern cricketers were made to bowl decent over-rates.

To me, Test cricket is the heart and soul of the game. Players are judged against each other and those of the past, and that is possible because those basic principles have not changed. But just because it has a history of almost 140 years, it doesn't mean Test cricket should be stuck in the past. I think we should look at the game and ask what can we do to make it better, more interesting and more relevant to today's world and still preserve the character and ethos of Test cricket.

Test match cricket has not changed for years, because traditionalists say it is a sacred cow and they want it to stay the same. They do not mind tinkering with Twenty20 and one-dayers, but Tests? Oh no, they are untouchable. Rubbish, what absolute nonsense!

It is a myth that today we are playing a traditional form of Test cricket that has spanned the history of the game.

Way back in the 1930s there was the occasional timeless Test, which I must say was quite ridiculous as the longest lasted for ten days, when England played South Africa in Durban. That match was abandoned as a draw only because England had a two-day rail journey to Cape Town to catch their ship home. Previously, the usual format was three-day Test matches, in the late 1930s it became four days and eventually they settled on five.

Through the 1960s and 1970s, when I played, we had a rest day in the middle of a Test match; the game would always start on a Thursday and we never played on the Sunday. What did we do on a rest day? Nothing. Often during a Test match in London, being the only northerner, I would be on my own. Players from Essex, Kent, Sussex, Surrey and Middlesex all went home on Saturday night to spend the next day with their families. A lot of the time, Michael Parkinson and his wife Mary would come to the Tests in London and take me back to their house in Bray and I would stay with them.

But cricket realised in the late 1980s that rest days were a thing of the past, fans were happy to go to the cricket on Sundays because life had changed and the Sunday observance laws relaxed. Now Tests can start on any day of the week. The Ashes series in England in 2013 even started on a Wednesday, instead of the traditional Thursday.

Even the length of an over has changed. Many years ago, there were three- or four-ball overs, and as I've mentioned in Australia they used to have eight-ball overs until it was standardised to the present-day six balls.

My point is that crowds are dwindling, but the men currently in charge appear blind to the problem and unable or unwilling to recognise it needs new ideas to encourage spectators back. Sometimes you have to be brave to embrace change and gamble.

On that England tour to Australia in 1970–71 we were 1–0 up in the Test series when the Melbourne Test match was abandoned without a ball being bowled due to rain. When it was announced the Test match had been called off, we agreed to play a one-day game instead and nearly 40,000 turned up, without prior tickets, and paid on the gate. The outfield was slippery and, not wanting to get anybody injured and jeopardise our chances of winning the Ashes (which we eventually did 2–0), we simply treated the game as we would a competitive exhibition match. So the first one-day international was played by accident. The first ball was bowled by Graham McKenzie, and I was the first batsman to receive a ball. I was also the first batsman ever to be out. There were not many rules specifically for that new format – we didn't have four men in the circle, coloured clothing or powerplays, and there was no strict interpretation of wides.

In fact, at that time nobody had even thought of one-day international cricket or day/night cricket. We didn't take that match seriously, as for us Test cricket was everything. Little did we know that this one-off fixture would revolutionise the game.

Over 20 years ago, I wrote that we should try day/night Test cricket in the hot countries and use coloured clothing. We should give the public a product that fits in with modern life. At the moment it is too tempting to stay at home. By watching on television, you do not have the inconvenience of travelling on a bus, tram or train to go to the match. Some will take their car and need to find a parking space, more often than not they will have quite a long walk to the ground and then have to queue up to get in. Sometimes there is the added frustration of a long wait while bags are searched on entry. After watching the day's play, you have most of this inconvenience again to travel home. This is something that the top officials and administrators of the game rarely experience. Maybe they should try it sometime!

People are also worried about taking time off work to watch cricket, because jobs are hard to find and even tougher to keep these days. Everyone seems to have to work harder for less money. We have to recognise that is what is happening in the real world and that as a consequence cricket is suffering.

I mentioned day/night Test cricket again in the Cowdrey Lecture. At the time Malcolm Speed, the chief executive of the ICC, pooh-poohed my idea, patronised me and condescendingly said: 'Well, that's just Geoffrey.' I thought he was a stupid prat! He just summed up some of the game's narrow-minded administrators.

It took the ICC another seven years to agree it was a good idea and give permission for countries to go ahead with day/night cricket, but not one country has been brave or adventurous enough to try it yet. They make excuses about the dew and a white ball, but that doesn't seem to matter when they all fall over themselves to have day/night one-dayers.

In countries where Test cricket is struggling, such as New Zealand, the UAE (where Pakistan now play), Sri Lanka, West Indies and South Africa, day/night Test cricket is the way forward, using the cerise pink ball invented and successfully trialled by the MCC, who have led the way on this issue. The ICC make up all sorts of pathetic excuses not to use it, I can only guess because it was not their idea in the first place. I know they are concerned about the viability of a pink ball lasting long enough during a day's play. But if they really had a strong desire to change Test cricket, they would come up with a plan. For example, why not use a different pink ball at each end so it would have to last for only 40 overs; it does not have to be 80 overs before it is changed. In 1948, when England played Australia, they changed the ball after 60 overs. It was a bit stupid on the part of England, mind you, because Australia had great fast bowlers in Ray Lindwall and Keith Miller and England lost the series 4–0.

In my experience, the ICC do not want any advice from anybody and have paid the MCC lip service because they are jealous to death of their reputation in the game. MCC have a huge standing and respect from when they ran world cricket and are still the caretakers of the laws of the game, like the R&A in golf. It appears there is a resentment towards the MCC by some at the ICC, but the old fuddy-duddies who used to run the game are long gone, the club has changed and the ICC should embrace the fact that the MCC could offer alternative leadership and ideas such as pushing for day/night Test cricket.

Playing at night-time is what sold Packer cricket. The first year of Packer cricket was a flop from the public point of view. In 1977–78 he held Super Tests between Australia and the Rest of the World and got just 14,000 people through the gate on day one. Over the three days in Sydney, only 24,000 turned up and Kerry Packer was shocked. Then one of his guys came up with the idea, after watching baseball in America, to use a white ball, coloured clothing, black sightscreens and play at night. Suddenly it took off and the grounds were full.

Anyone who lives in Australia or South Africa knows when it is hot you want to get up early and go to work. It is not like freezing your balls off in an England winter when you don't want to get out of bed. They go to work early and finish at three then go to the beach or play golf. If Tests started mid-afternoon, then they could pick up the kids after school and make an evening at the Test a family outing. That way you are giving the public a product that fits around their lives. And if we have more kids coming through the gate, we should also give them what they want.

I am a traditionalist and I want to see Test cricketers wearing white. But I am old, young kids love coloured clothing, so the kit could be predominantly white with some colour on it and the players' names on the back. Children love to wear their favourite player's shirt and think they are superstars like their idol. All the jazz that goes with Twenty20 could be transferred to Test cricket, as long as we do not mess around with the fundamentals of the game.

I am not advocating radical changes in the format of Tests. I don't want to see the pitch shortened from 22 yards or a fourth stump added – that would be silly. It would also be unnecessary, because the cricket is so entertaining these days at Test level that if we market the game properly and play it at times when people can watch it then it will survive. The game has always evolved, if there is forward thinking and a strong desire then you can do anything.

Then we come to the problem in England of cricket not being shown on terrestrial television. Many families cannot afford to buy satellite, so they are denied the opportunity of seeing any form of live cricket on television and can't go to the matches because it is too expensive, with the best tickets costing about £100, meaning some pay more than a pound to watch an over. I am not anti-Sky. I started my commentary career with Sky and worked for them for six wonderful years. I loved it. They are brilliant at showing cricket, but I would only sell a portion of our cricket to satellite and some to terrestrial.

The ECB were seduced by Sky's money and say it props up the game and among other things keeps the counties solvent. But it is a vicious circle. The counties are not stupid and know they are storing up danger for the future by not having cricket on terrestrial television. They are aware that vast swathes of the next generation will not grow up, like I did, thinking cricket is our summer game. But they dare not vote to give cricket back to terrestrial television because the reduction in their money would finish off certain counties.

The ECB insisted a few years ago that all the Test grounds should have better drainage, floodlights and recommended the need for a certain amount of covered seating. This all costs the grounds concerned huge amounts of money, which most can only raise by borrowing from the banks. They then have to make enough money to pay back those loans and cover the interest. They are in trouble because of these debts, so whenever television comes in and offers lots of money, the counties are happy because it helps ease their financial problems. They will vote for the chairman at the ECB who can get the big, fat TV contracts.

The county officials are trapped in a catch-22 situation. Take Yorkshire as an example. I joined the board in 2005. On a turnover of £7 million per year, after running costs we had about £1 million surplus, and out of that approximately £700,000 was needed to service the loans. Now that interest payment has gone up to £1.2 million, so in eight years Yorkshire have to find an extra £500,000 a year, just to stand still.

It is down to necessary investment in the ground. Yorkshire built a big pavilion and got a gift of £12 million from Leeds Carnegie University, but there was still the cost of kitting it out and its ongoing maintenance. Now the club has to install those floodlights by the end of 2019, otherwise the ECB will not allocate any more international cricket to Headingley. Those floodlights will cost £1.8 million and the ECB will furnish £700,000 towards them, but that still leaves the club having to find over a million pounds. There is a spider's web of debt, as each county is desperate for money every year just to stay afloat.

Many of our Test match grounds base their borrowing and forward planning on holding a match involving England, otherwise they are in financial trouble. It means all are reluctant to rock the boat with the ECB and do not complain about the lack of cricket on terrestrial television, but they should because their own attendances are being hit, too.

When I played in the 1960s, we would play matches all over Yorkshire but now it has had to become centralised, because of costs, taking the game away from those who do not live in the big towns or cities. Counties now play at their main grounds and live day-to-day on the £2 million-plus handouts from the ECB. That is the pot generated by England rights sold to television, plus sponsorship and perimeter advertising. Even the other counties that do not have an international ground are in debt and need their share of ECB money to survive. But the problem is I can't see county clubs surviving for the next 20–30 years simply on the central handouts.

There have been suggestions that some counties should amalgamate, but how do you say which one stays or goes? It is like having twins and keeping only one: who is going to make that decision? There will be huge resistance and all are scared even to contemplate it. Instead, it will be down to market forces who survives, and some will go out of business – I don't know which ones, it could be Yorkshire for all I know. When I played for them in the 1970s, we had 13,000 members, now the club are lucky to attract even half that number. More spectators used to come to watch me have a net before start of play than now turn up at some county matches.

How long can the television money keep the 18 counties afloat? They are all in debt and the debts are getting bigger, so the pot has to keep getting bigger. Administrators will tell you they care, make all the right noises but a lot of politicians do that as well and we don't believe them either. Some administrators don't care what happens in the future, because they know it will not happen on their watch as they will be dead, retired or will have moved on to another job. When it all goes wrong, it will be someone else's problem to deal with, not theirs.

CHAPTER 10

ASHES DISASTER

In the summer of 2013 England won the Ashes with ease, but a few months later supporters were dumbfounded when Australia gained revenge with a stunning whitewash on their home soil. England fans were left asking: how did that happen? Well, there were many reasons which combined to produce a result that ripped apart English cricket, costing Andy Flower his job as coach and the sacking of Kevin Pietersen.

England were stunned by an Australia side that wanted to win more than they did. Australia were desperate to regain the Ashes after a period of English dominance and for many Australia players it was their last chance to taste Ashes glory. If Australia had lost at home and conceded the Ashes for a fourth consecutive time, they would have been crucified by their media. We have seen how the Australia press give England stick, but it is doubled when they turn on their own team. The Australian public would also have given the players hell. It would have been an impossible time for the likes of Michael Clarke and senior players such as Shane Watson and Brad Haddin, who would have been forever tainted with Ashes failure.

This burning desire to win was in contrast to England, who thought because they had beaten Australia three times in succession they would be able to go Down Under, defend the Ashes and make history by being the first English team to win four series in a row. In other words, they were complacent. But Andy Flower had failed to spot his team were in decline, or did not want to believe that players who had performed well for him in the past were fading away.

England did not rate the Aussie batsmen; many thought Chris Rogers was past it, Watson was always getting out lbw and Haddin was over the hill. They only really respected Clarke, and were probably a little bit wary of David Warner's aggression, but felt the others offered no real threat.

England beat Australia in the winter of 2010–11 under Andrew Strauss on their own pitches quite comfortably, and then won 3–0 in the summer of 2013 without playing particularly well. Our players got sucked in to believing their own publicity and thought they could just go over there and do it again. Everything would be all right on the day. They were completely wrong and had been blind to the signs that had been building for a year. When England batted in New Zealand in March 2013 and against Australia in the summer that followed, they failed to compile big first-innings scores. It is the first innings that controls a Test match; if you can make a large total then, you can dictate to the opposition.

We did not do that. England struggled against New Zealand because our batsmen were making elementary, silly mistakes due to over-confidence. They were getting themselves out and were lucky to escape with a draw, clinging on by one wicket in the final Auckland Test when New Zealand should really have beaten us.

Following on from that, England appeared to thump Australia 3–0 but the result flattered them. England should have lost the first Test match at Trent Bridge, but were lucky Stuart Broad was given not out off his glove, a poor umpiring decision that cost Australia the match. Australia should have won the third Test at Manchester; they set England an impossible target of 332 to win in the fourth innings and they were 32 for three when it rained on the last day, causing the match to be abandoned. The series should really have been 2–2.

England would have retained the Ashes, but such a result might have made the team and coaching staff sit up and take notice. A dose of reality would have done them some good and they may have addressed the issues which became major problems in Australia.

The appointment of Darren Lehmann immediately before the Tests in England started was a surprise, but it changed the dynamic between the two sides. I know from first-hand experience of him at Yorkshire that he is a very ebullient, confident, aggressive, in-your-face type of individual. His arrival certainly made me think the Ashes could be interesting. But in England Darren had inherited Mickey Arthur's squad and had no say or input with the Australian selectors as to the individuals already picked for the tour or those left out. His only real change was to bring in Steve Smith, which became a good selection. Smith was languishing on the Australia A tour to England, but repaid Lehmann's confidence with a century in The Oval Test before making two more hundreds in the winter return series.

Mitchell Johnson had not been selected to play the English summer against England, but Lehmann chose him for the one-day series and it proved to be a masterstroke. With that selection Lehmann outflanked his opposite number, Andy Flower, who has to accept the blame for overlooking the threat Johnson could pose in the winter. Andy was no longer directly involved in the coaching of the one-day side, having given that up the previous year to Ashley Giles. It meant he did not watch Johnson carefully enough in the one-day series and neither did the batting coach, Graham Gooch. If I saw what was happening – why didn't they?

They failed to spot that Johnson was bowling really fast and straight. He caused problems for our batsmen by getting the ball up quickly with lots of lift from just short of a length and was very accurate. He was hitting them on the glove and making them duck and weave. The only reason Johnson did not take a hatful of wickets is because in one-day cricket, unlike Tests, there is hardly anybody around the bat to take catches as the fielders are spread out to save runs. In Australia three years previously, Johnson had, to say the least, been really poor. He'd sprayed it everywhere and was not a danger to anybody except the wicketkeeper, diving all over the place to save his stray balls down the leg side. Apart from one good Test in Perth, when it all clicked for him and he took nine wickets in the match, he was fast but wild.

The Barmy Army wrote a song about him:

He bowls it to the left, he bowls it to the right,

That Mitchell Johnson,

His bowling is shite.

They were singing that in good heart with England winning and when he was bowling poorly. He reacted badly to all the jeering from the Barmy Army and lost his confidence. He later admitted the Barmy Army song rattled him and he would even sing it to himself at the top of his bowling mark, which shows how much they had got under his skin.

There is no point bowling quickly if you cannot control the direction. Sheer speed alone does not get wickets and Johnson's career was in decline. But I always thought he could end up having the last laugh because raw speed, when harnessed properly, wins matches. Before he returned for the one-day series in England, Johnson worked for some time with Terry Alderman and Dennis Lillee, two great bowlers from his adopted home state of Western Australia. They lengthened his run and got his leading arm higher. He was back in the groove. He hit Jonathan Trott on the helmet and on the gloves a number of times and a few other batsmen were made to look uncomfortable.

If Andy Flower had taken the time to watch that carefully, he would have realised there was a big problem brewing but he failed to notice Johnson had suddenly rediscovered his touch. A coach does not bat and make runs, or bowl and take wickets, his job is to watch, plan and prepare.

He should have seen the improvement of Johnson and noted what damage he could do in Test matches on hard, bouncy Australian pitches when he is allowed to bowl an unlimited amount of overs, rather than the maximum of ten in one-day cricket. Add in slips, gully and short leg, and suddenly Johnson becomes a real threat, particularly as modern batsmen are not comfortable with the ball zipping around their noses. Today's players are simply not used to facing genuine pace. The days of the West Indies having four big, nasty, quick bowlers are long gone. A lot of England's work should have been done before they left for Australia.

In 1990 Graham Gooch was an England player when Mickey Stewart, the head coach, asked me to work with the England batsmen to prepare them for the upcoming tour to the West Indies. Goochie had endured a miserable summer getting out cheaply a number of times to Terry Alderman during the Ashes series. I knew they were not going to play any spinners or face many nice juicy half volleys. They would be facing fast bowlers from both ends banging it in short.

I worked with the batsmen in the nets at Headingley with two cameras to film the action. One was positioned at point, the other behind the bowler's arm. We had a big quick bowler called Tony, who bowled in the Yorkshire leagues, come in to help. I told him to bowl off 20 yards, bang it in short and knock their blocks off. That is what he did, because bowling two yards through the crease gave him the same pace you would face in Test cricket. Our players would come up for sessions every two weeks and very quickly they were grumbling like mad in the changing rooms about all the short stuff I was giving them.

Nasser Hussain had a beautiful off drive, inside out through the covers, but I stopped him after four balls and said: 'Listen, you are four for three. You have nicked all four to the slips.

They have caught three and you might be lucky that one has gone between fourth slip and gully for four.'

I would keep stopping the session and we would study the video together and then go back for more practice. I showed the players how to duck and weave and defend well, a process that would wear the fast bowlers down. If you can't defend you are never in. Eventually they became comfortable with all the short balls and went to the West Indies and won the first Test. The second was abandoned and they would have won the third Test in Trinidad, but were cheated out of it by West Indies bowling their overs slow and bad light.

Had I been in charge before England left for Australia, recognising the threat of Johnson, I would have insisted that the England batsmen did some work in the indoor nets to get used to the speed and the left-arm angle Johnson creates. They may have sent Tymal Mills from Essex and Harry Gurney from Notts, two left-arm seamers, to bowl at them in the nets in Perth at the start of the tour before the Test series, but it was too late by then.

Having left-arm seamers for practice helps you get used to Johnson's angle, but it does not prepare for his extra pace and hostility. Instead of bowling line and length, Goochie should have remembered how I had prepared them for the West Indies tour. Mills and Gurney needed to bowl through the crease and inflict the threat of physical injury on our players. That is the only way to get mentally prepared for what is coming, the more you face short-pitched stuff the more accomplished you become at it; suddenly it does not frighten you anymore. Conquer the fear of getting hurt and you are halfway there.

A fast bowler tests your character by bowling short and making you duck and weave. If you survive the barrage, he will eventually pitch one up and then you hit it. In between times you have to play the quicks well to send them a message. Fast bowlers are unstoppable when they get on a roll. But what you have to remember is that fast bowlers usually bowl only in short spells, perhaps four or five overs at a time, so they can make the most of their energy in explosive bursts. Your plan should be to break their spell down in your mind to four overs, 24 balls. Probably six of those balls will be bouncers down the leg or off side. You can duck and weave and not really play at those balls. Then we have 18 balls left between two batsmen, which is really only nine balls each. In other words see him off. Surely Goochie was telling his batsman this. If not, then he was not doing his job properly.

In other words, you try to lessen his impact. But if you have not done your preparation properly, then you do not know how to see him off and you have no chance. For me Andy's failure to sort that out was a huge factor and the stats bear it out. At the end of the series Johnson had 37 wickets at 13.97. In the last 25 years or so, that is the best by a fast bowler.

You have to go back to 1881–92 to match his performance. In a ten-year period, George Lohmann of Surrey, a seam bowler, played 18 Test matches and took 112 wickets at 10.75. That was on uncovered pitches of poor quality when it was easier to take wickets. Now it is much harder for bowlers. Most historians and many ex-players who are students of the game regard S.F. Barnes as the greatest bowler ever. He played 27 Test matches for England and took 189 wickets at 16.43. Johnson bowled on modern, flat decks and still his record matched the

great bowlers of the earlier eras. It was a remarkable performance, but we helped him along the way by lacking a cohesive
strategy.

What you have to do at Test level, and I know a bit about it
having played a lot of great fast bowlers, is be able to work the
ones and twos. You have to have soft hands and an ability to
turn the wrists so you can deflect the ball in to little gaps. This
frustrates bowlers into trying something new, which then forces
them to bowl you a hittable ball. That is your life-blood against
great bowlers. It keeps you going through the hard times, and
takes the pressure off.

Andy should have known his history. Fast bowlers win Test
matches, particularly Ashes series in Australia. In 1932–33
Harold Larwood put Bodyline into operation and did all the
damage, even cutting down the great Don Bradman's batting
by half. In 1954–55, on Len Hutton's tour of Australia, Frank
Tyson won the series with help from Brian Statham and Trevor
Bailey. There were a number of occasions when Keith Miller
and Ray Lindwall destroyed England, with big Bill Johnson
also a real threat as back-up. In 1974–75 Australia blew us away
with Lillee and Thomson.

History tells us when you have a great fast bowler, you have
an ace to trump anything the opposition have. No contest.
Gooch was a close colleague of mine. He was an opening partner, a terrific batsman and a really good guy. At the end of the
Ashes series he was right to say: 'We all need to have a good
look at ourselves after this performance.' I am glad Graham
Gooch was honest and said everybody had to share the blame.
But was he giving them the right advice or was it a case of them
not listening? If he was giving them poor advice, then he was

failing in his job. If they were not listening, then either the players or the coach has to go.

All through Australia I watched my friend Goochie working with our batsmen. I saw him giving them a lot of throw-downs with the sidearm throwing aid that dog walkers use to pick up a ball and hurl it long distances for the dog to fetch. That's all well and good, but it is not how I see the batting coach's job. The guys loved the fact that Graham was prepared to do the donkey work and took time to help them in that way, but my brother or any member of the Barmy Army could give throw-downs using that stick. For me, coaching is studying the technique of the batsmen under you, helping them tidy up in defence and talking to them about where and how to play certain bowlers. It is about explaining to them that on different pitches against certain bowlers some scoring areas are risky. Point out the scoring areas that offer higher reward for lower risk. In other words, at the top level it is about teaching the art of scoring runs and arming batsmen with the know-how to exploit weaknesses in the bowlers.

There was no shame in losing wickets to Johnson, but what really annoyed me was England had no plan against Nathan Lyon, the off-spinner bowling on flat pitches around the wicket to our right-handers. In eight Test matches, three in England and five in Australia, he took 28 wickets at 30 and we did not improve one iota against his bowling. He is a decent spinner, but he is not Jim Laker and he does not bowl a 'doosra' that can confuse you like Muttiah Muralitharan or Saeed Ajmal. He is an orthodox finger spinner who bowled around the wicket, and that should be straightforward for Test-standard batsmen, but our guys stayed back, crease-bound like flies caught in a spider's web. Our right-handers did not move. They were too scared to use their feet and go down the pitch. They were stuck in the crease, waiting for a bad, short ball to cut. It was like he was bowling hand grenades to them all the time and they were fearful the ball would explode.

In Test cricket you get very few bad balls from a good spinner, so England were reduced to playing sweeps off the stumps, which are fraught with great danger if you miss the ball, especially with the Decision Review System (DRS) giving spinners a lot more lbws these days. The other option is to try to hit him over the top and clear the in-field, but that is very risky if you take the shot on when you have not been in very long. You have not had time to judge the surface, the turn and flight through the air.

The job of the coach is to talk to batsmen in the nets and work out how to counter someone like Lyon. If you talk to better players around the world, or even to Darren Lehmann and ask him what he told the Australia players, you will find out what their policy is towards spinners. On modern, flat pitches if it does not spin then a good batting team should not allow an orthodox finger spinner to tie up one end. He should be batted out of the attack, which is exactly what Australia did to Graeme Swann. When it turns then it is different, you have to be more patient.

After seeing how our batsmen struggled against Lyon in three Tests in England, we should have worked on getting to the pitch of the ball and driving it to mid off and mid on for ones or twos. Cut out the risky shots and take the easy runs on offer. If our guys had picked him off down the ground, the scoreboard would have ticked over and Lyon would have become frustrated by the fact they were playing him easily. OK, you would not be smacking him around, but he would start to experiment and give you the odd poor ball to drive or hit off the back foot through the covers.

But for that to happen, our right-handed batsmen needed the confidence from working on their technique to get the feet moving rather than becoming bogged down. It is like playing chess. You move the pawns first to get in a good position to bring your big guns, the bishops, knights and rooks, into play. Finally you can start moving your biggest piece, the queen. To play chess well, you need to be able to think and plan ahead. It is the same for a batsman in Test cricket. It is about strategy, but instead we allowed Lyon to dictate to us in eight Test matches. All the batsmen were at fault, and nobody escapes criticism apart from the young boy Ben Stokes, who made a marvellous century in his second Test at Perth. But as for the rest, it was a tour of shame.

I could not believe opening batsman Michael Carberry's foot-work. He was rooted on the back foot to the quicks, and only came forward to play a flashing off drive. His problem, and this would have been an issue in England as well, was he never got his front foot past the batting crease. Whenever he played forward in an attempt to smother the ball, he was still stuck on the batting crease, so he was miles away from the pitch of the ball. I am sorry but that kind of fundamentally poor footwork will always get him in trouble against top-class bowlers. If he is going to wait for a four ball to play with a flashing off drive, then he needs enormous patience when batting against top-class attacks, and Australia gave England very few bad balls to whack. It is not like county cricket where bowlers make more mistakes.

Joe Root was no better. He lost his footwork and became almost scoreless, frightened to play an attacking shot. In my opinion, he was picked too early by England. At the time various selectors asked me for my opinion and I told them that one day he will be a superb player and play for many years for our country. I saw him at Yorkshire and I felt that when he got in he had the composure, confidence, concentration and wide range of shots to make superb centuries, but he struggled against the new ball early on and was not yet ready. He had one good season for Yorkshire, who were in the Second Division at the time, and was then thrust on to the international stage.

In only 16 Test matches, before being dropped for the Sydney Test, he was shunted up and down the order from No.1 to No.6. He has played one-day and Twenty20 cricket for England as well, so I am not surprised that someone like him, lacking in first-class experience, lost his footwork in Australia. When he played forward to the seamers, he never moved his foot out to the pitch of the ball. He was stuck on the crease every time. He is good enough to correct this problem through some quality time in the nets, but not while he keeps playing Twenty20 cricket. He needs to get some good coaching and play first-class cricket without having to slog the ball around in one-dayers.

Root is young and still learning, but Alastair Cook is one of the best in the world and Australia's planning and preparation for our captain were a lesson to England. They identified his strengths and exploited his weaknesses. Cook lost confidence and his footwork because Australia kept the ball off his pads, which has always been his bread and butter shot. If it is on his legs pitched up, then he tucks it away comfortably. If it is short-ish on his hip, he pulls it and he cuts anything short and wide on the off side. But Australia gave him nothing on his legs or any short balls to cut. They bowled it full and across him all the time. It did not matter to Australia if the ball was wide and he didn't play at it, because it meant he was not scoring runs. He was not able to get going and they kept bowling it wide to tempt him, because they knew it would play on his mind that he was not scoring.

The off drive is fraught with danger against quality fast bowlers with the new ball such as Johnson, Ryan Harris and Peter Siddle. By cutting off his normal area of scoring, Australia forced him to try shots he was not comfortable with and the result was inevitable. It ate away at Cook's confidence and in the end you saw a bloody good batsman out of form. In Adelaide he even hooked at Johnson and got caught at fine leg, something he never does. They scrambled his brain to such a point he was playing at balls wide of off-stump without moving his feet. Australia were pulling him left, right and centre.

I would have explained this excellent Australian strategy to him and told him to stick to his game plan and not go outside his comfort zone. This would require more patience than he had ever had to use in the past and would mean scoring slower against the new ball. But he needed to win the battle against the new ball even at the cost of scoring slowly, then once he had worn the bowlers down, and the ball got older, he could gain momentum. This would not be easy or eye-catching, but it was a better option than playing poor shots and being dismissed cheaply.

Off the field it was just as bad for England. Very few people knew or suspected Jonathan Trott had a problem. After he went home Flower admitted they had been managing his illness for some time. He said: 'I was first aware that Jonathan struggled with these things from our first contact as player and coach. He's been managing it from the start of the tour and there was no reason to suggest that this Test should be any different.'

Now hang on. If you have got some kind of depression or mental health issue, which a lot of people do not understand, and I admit I am one of them, does it not mean you have a ticking time bomb on your hands? At some stage it was going to go off. England have had experience of this before, so they have no excuse. Marcus Trescothick, a bloody fine batsman in one-day cricket and Tests, had his issues which have been well documented. Mike Yardy, a moderate player, came home from the World Cup in Sri Lanka in 2011, again with the coaching staff saying they were 'managing' his situation.

We have had two episodes before, so they should have known at some stage Trott's problem may become so great he would not be able to carry on. Until then, Trott had had continued success and this was his first real crisis. There was always a danger his condition would explode, which is more likely to happen when you are under pressure, such as when you have been hammered in the first Test of an Ashes series away from home. England lost badly in Brisbane, and Trott played Johnson poorly, having struggled against him in the one-day series a few weeks previously. It was stress and pressure. It is the name of the game for top sportsmen. You cannot avoid it; it is the nature of our job. Test match cricket has always been about whether you can handle the pressure.

Having an individual with a stress-related illness begs the question of whether he should have been in the team in the first place. England will say he had a lot of success in the past, but it seems to me that it is when people are not doing well that the stress takes over. Yardy had been dropped and was struggling before he went home with illness. It appears that it manifests itself in failure, and bad performances exacerbate any existing problems. You never see players going home with depression illnesses when they are scoring lots of runs or taking wickets.

England then made a mess of replacing Trott. They unwisely promoted Root up the order, when he did not have the technique to cope with the quick bowlers, and waited until the final Test before finally batting Ian Bell at three. Mind you, he did little better than Root.

Bell is a guy with everything. He has so much talent; he is a modern-day, right-handed David Gower. He is so elegant, batting is effortless and he has superb timing with a wide range of shots on front and back foot, but I get the impression he does not use his brain, and just plays naturally. If it comes off he looks great, if it doesn't he just shrugs his shoulders and moves on to the next knock. Sadly, England are not blessed with many quality batsmen who can replace Bell, so he gets away with nonchalant dismissals, such as his first baller in the second innings of the Melbourne Test, when England were looking to build on a first-innings lead and actually had a chance to win the match.

Bell came in at 86 for three and England were wobbling again. What did he do? First ball he spooned a catch to mid off. He just punched it head high; it was the most thoughtless shot you could imagine. I hope the coaching staff gave him hell for that, but even if they did it must have fallen on deaf ears.

Ian came in at Sydney in the fifth Test with England struggling in the second innings. Johnson had destroyed us for four Test matches and was on a roll again. Bell had hardly been at the crease when he tried to uppercut very fast short balls from Johnson. He did not play himself in or try to see off Johnson. His team were in trouble, but he played his own way. He missed the first uppercut, finally made contact with one and scored a four through third man. Australia then set the trap by putting a fielder at third man. What did Bell do? He tried it again. Luckily it went for six over the fielder's head. I was asking myself: what was he thinking? If Bell had been caught he would have looked stupid and a mug like his team-mate KP in Perth. This was the type of thoughtless batting that cost us the Ashes.

Then we have to look at the bowling. David Saker, the fast bowling coach, admirably admitted that he was at fault for Steven Finn's problems. He said: 'It's disappointing and I take quite a bit of responsibility because my job is to get him playing well for England and that hasn't worked the way we would have liked.'

That is a start. At least someone was bold enough to put their hand up and admit they made a mistake. I applaud Saker for that. We all make mistakes, but this was a big one because I believe Steven Finn is the best fast bowling prospect we have had for years. They ruined him with all the fiddling about with his action and delivery. He had been taking four and a half wickets per Test with an average per wicket of 29.40, which is acceptable for the modern game. You cannot take wickets like they did in the 1950s, 60s and 70s; nowadays it is harder for bowlers like Finn because the pitches are covered. Modern bats hit the ball further than ever before and the ball flies over the super-smooth outfields, while boundaries are a lot shorter too.

My view is we just let him bowl. Tell him to get the ball from his end, down to the other end and take wickets and stop filling his head with advice. His habit of knocking the stumps over at the non-striker's end with his back leg has led to a slump. When the ICC decided that in such situations the umpire had to call a no-ball, Finn felt he had to change his technique. But who the hell cares if he clips the stumps at the non-striker's end and there are five or six no-balls called per day? Those runs will make no difference, but the wickets he takes can win Test matches. England spent too long concentrating on altering all sorts of things, his run-up, approach to the crease and the point of release, that he forgot how to bowl.

He spent two and a half months in Australia working with the bowling coach, but in the end they did not dare pick him, even for the one-dayers. England should be ashamed about what happened to Finn, and Andy Flower should never have allowed it to go so far. It was pathetic. They should have sent him home at the end of the Ashes series to rest and recuperate and then picked him for the Lions tour to Sri Lanka, where he could have bowled away from the spotlight and rediscovered some confidence. Instead they compounded the problem. Saker left Finn in a mess and Ashley Giles, the one-day coach, then sent him home saying he was 'not selectable'. The lad had been out there having nets for two and a half months and he was now 'not selectable'. Enduring that embarrassment must have been hugely demoralising for the kid.

Steven was one of the three giant fast bowlers picked for the tour, in the belief they would scare the life out of Australian batsmen. It was one of the biggest selection blunders in modern English cricket. Andy was part of the selection process, along with Geoff Miller (the former chairman of selectors), Ashley Giles and James Whitaker, who has since been promoted to chief selector. They were all responsible and must share the blame. In fact, while England were being hammered, Geoff was picking up a gong in the New Year's Honours List, unfortunate timing to say the least.

Boyd Rankin was not good enough or fit enough, Finn had been cocked up by the coaches and Chris Tremlett was a yard down on pace. The mistake with Tremlett went back further than the Ashes tour. Andy Flower was one of the selectors who did not pick him for the fifth Ashes Test at The Oval in the summer. That was a mistake. If he had played we would have seen he had lost pace, which was exactly the message we were getting from people who had seen him bowl in county cricket.

It was three years since he had done well in Australia. That is a very long time for a fast bowler. He had also suffered a number of injuries since then and Andy should have tested him out before taking him on such a big Ashes tour, but instead England picked Chris Woakes rather than Tremlett. Woakes is a nice county cricketer who would have done well years ago when Test matches were played on uncovered pitches and there was a bit of grass to help seam bowlers. He can bat, too. But today's pitches are better prepared, have better covering and marvellous drainage so they are flatter than ever before. There is not so much joy for medium pacers like Woakes. You need genuine pace and he does not have it. He played at The Oval because Flower wanted to look at the young spinner

Simon Kerrigan, which left them needing Woakes's batting ability.

But Kerrigan was embarrassing and Cook did not dare bowl him. He did not use his front arm at all in delivery and looked like a club bowler. That was a monumental blunder and a harbinger of things to come in Australia. The selectors, and Andy, should be ashamed of themselves for those two calls.

With Tremlett and the experiment of picking three giant fast bowlers failing, England needed their senior spin bowler, Graeme Swann, to perform but his retirement in the middle of the series in Australia was a bitter blow.

I watched him very carefully in the three Test matches he played and I could see the ball was not coming out of his hand the right way when he bowled. He has always had flight and guile with good spin. In Australia, he was always going to have few opportunities to spin the ball because of the harder, flatter pitches, so flight and control were vital. Spinners have to bowl a number of balls in the same area, three or four, and then try something different to tempt a batsman with a wider delivery or one flighted with more air. They alter their line and length to take a wicket, but it was quite clear to me Swann could no longer do that.

He could not land it where he wanted. I could see what he was thinking. Every time he tried to tempt the batsman, it failed. The ball was not landing on the right length or on the right line. His control had deserted him. On top of that, the Aussies had a great plan to target him. They did not allow him to settle and tie them down. Remember, England's cricket for a long time had been based on three fast bowlers who could alternate and stay fresh while Swann bowled a lot of overs at one end. Swann's excellent bowling over a number of years allowed our seamers to rest between spells. He would seal up one end by being both a wicket-taking bowler and someone who could also strangle the run rate. It meant the opposition hardly ever got on top of him and the quicks very rarely had to be over-bowled.

Swann was not the same after his elbow operation in the spring of 2013. OK, he had a successful summer against Australia that year, taking 26 wickets at 29, his best series return, but the pitches were so doctored in his favour he could not fail. His problem with his elbow was covered up by those slow, low turning surfaces. Even though he did not have the same flight and guile, he could extract turn and Australians are poor players of a spinning ball. He perhaps thought any problems with his elbow would clear up by playing more cricket, while the opportunity to be in an England team that could win four Ashes series on the trot was too tempting to pass up.

But the magic had gone, and it was noticeable when he retired after the third Test in Perth that he admitted his elbow had never been the same after the operation earlier that year. I am glad he was honest and gave up the game when he realised he could no longer perform. It must have been a terrible decision to have to make. He must have been so deflated when he realised his zip had gone forever and he would never get it back. At that moment I can understand why he walked away and could not face bowling another ball. You just want to run away, hide and get out of the limelight.

I'm sure it hit him hard. Australia coming at him on pitches where it did not turn must have made it worse. I believe Andy Flower and Alastair Cook tried to talk him out of retirement, but his mind was made up. He was smiling on television when he gave his last press conference, but deep down Swann would have been hurting terribly. It must have been tearing him apart to know he was not the bowler he used to be and he was getting slaughtered like he was in Perth, when his last over was smashed for 22 by Shane Watson.

It was fair enough that he decided he could no longer play, but it would have been better had he stayed on with the tour. It was obvious Monty Panesar was going to play in Melbourne and he perhaps could have done with some advice from Swann. If Swann had helped carry the drinks, it would have been a great sign of togetherness; instead he wasn't given that option. Graeme says Andy Flower told him if you can't play then you have to go home. Swanny had his wife and two small children out there on holiday, so was stuck trying to find flights and accommodation. Kevin Pietersen helped him out and spoke to a friend in Dubai, who fixed them up with a motel. It's not surprising he departed with a wisecrack about players being 'up their own arses' and handed the Aussie press another stick with which to beat England.

Swann had been a star player for five years, during which time all the reserve players had carried drinks for him. It would have shown a lot of character to stay on and help the team in the background, and then announced his retirement when he went home. He would have earned more respect if he had seen the tour out. It is not as if he would have got in the way. There are so many backroom staff with an England squad these days that it is like a mini-army touring the world.

Under Andy England over-complicated professionalism. There were about 16 backroom staff in Australia. How do you get

16 backroom staff in the dressing room? If I had been a player, I would have been telling a few of them to get lost and give me some space. If you have coaches for everything – analysts on laptops showing you where opposition players hit the ball and a psychologist telling you what you should and should not be thinking – then players stop working things out for themselves.

They were even told what to eat. Before the series started, the Australian press got hold of an 82-page document sent to all the Test grounds in Australia by the ECB to tell them what food to prepare for the players and send to the dressing room at the end of play. Somebody at the ECB had decided foods such as mungbean curry, piri-piri breaded tofu, goji berries and quinoa was good for the players. The menus were designed by Chris Rosimus, the ECB's performance nutritionist. He wrote in the booklet: 'Some ingredients within this book will not be in season when you come to use them. If availability is an issue, please do not use an alternative or omit from the recipe. Please feel free [unless specified] to serve the sandwiches on any variety of bread you wish. However, a preference would be whole wheat, seeded or rye varieties. For any meat used in sandwich fillings, please do not use processed meats, only freshly cooked meats will suffice.'

What a load of rubbish. Can this Chris Rosimus bat or bowl? Does he take any wickets or score any runs? Has he stood in the field all day for six hours in searing heat? That 82-page document made the team a laughing stock before a ball was bowled. The Aussie media had a fine old time deriding us before we started. It was embarrassing and unnecessary. Whoever thought that was a good thing to send to Australia wants his head testing.

If it was Andy trying to be very professional, then it was misguided. If he did not know about it, then he should have denounced it immediately so the team did not get ridiculed in the media. It does not matter if the person who wrote the booklet got upset. I don't know why he had been employed in the first place.

There have been a lot of great cricketers who have lived on eating hamburgers and smoking cigarettes. Look at Shane Warne. He is the best example of all. I love his bowling, his character and everything about him. I wish I had played against him. What a fabulous cricketer and personality. He loves hamburgers and ciggies, but his diet did not stop him taking 708 Test wickets.

And then we come to the team psychologist, Dr Mark Bawden. Apparently he was with the team during the warm-up games in Australia until the first Test in Brisbane. No offence to the guy, but in a team sport players should be talking things over with each other and working things out together, that is what a team is for. The best motto is the three musketeers' 'All for one, and one for all.'

I would not let a psychologist near my team. I first heard he was on the tour while commentating for *Test Match Special* with Simon Mann, my BBC colleague. I asked: 'Why do they need a psychoanalyst?' Simon explained perhaps he helps the players relax before a big event.

I said: 'Jesus, before going in to bat, I didn't need to be relaxed and calm. At the moment of playing in a big game, I want my senses to be sharpened. I want everything in my body alert and ready to move fast. As soon as I go into bat, I will be dealing in fractions of seconds against fast bowlers trying to knock my block off or get me out. I need to move quickly. I need to have feet that are dancing and moving on my toes, because the ball is coming at me at over ninety mph. Calm? Low? Sleepy? No thank you.'

When you play top-level sport you need to have nervous energy; apprehension is good for all of us. The best players are all nervous. Before a big match and going out to bat, if someone tells you they are not nervous then they are either a liar or an idiot. It is about controlling that nervous energy in a positive way.

The best example I can give is my old friend Dickie Bird. I played with him at Barnsley when I was 15. He is five years older than me and he was the star. He used to come to me before going out to bat shaking like a leaf. He would say: 'Put my gloves on for me, Gerald.' I would remind him that my name was Geoffrey, and he would say: 'Right, put my gloves on, Gerald!'

He was that nervous he could not perform. He was OK at club level, but in county cricket his nerves got the better of him. But then he became the best umpire I ever played under. He could control his nervous energy to make the fewest mistakes and lots of good decisions. It helped him handle players brilliantly with a great sense of humour, and not in a schoolmasterly way.

England's reliance on sports psychologists goes far deeper than just the senior side. The ECB's performance psychology team, for that is what they are called, is five strong. They have James Bell working with the Under-18s team, Simon Crampton with the England women's academy and Bawden with the England side. Amanda Gatherer is the clinical psychologist and Dr Wil James the national lead, whatever that means.

When you read this, it is amazing. If the ECB and Andy believe this psychologist stuff is so important, then why did Bawden not stay with the team for the whole tour? Mark Bawden is quoted as saying: 'We very rarely talk about winning. It's pretty unhelpful, really.' He also goes on to say: 'No, we wouldn't talk about losing.' I read that and could not believe my eyes. When you play sport it is competitive; winning and losing are the outcomes, they are what it is all about. But he is saying they do not want to focus on the end result. They want to concentrate 'on our processes'. Sorry. This is mumbo jumbo.

I can't judge Bawden on his successes, because we do not know who he has been dealing with. But presumably I can judge him on Trott, and his advice did not prevent Jonathan crumbling. I do accept the medical profession has moved forward and taken huge steps since my playing days, but I know after 50 years of playing and watching cricket that the best players never needed all this help. Years ago, it was seen as a weakness if you had to go to a 'quack', as we called psychologists, and we would not want to go see one because of the stigma. If you were struggling and out of form, lacking confidence, dispirited or your demeanour was down, your team-mates would say 'pull yourself together'. We actually thought playing top sport was about being mentally strong and not just about ability.

Look at Mark Ramprakash: he was technically excellent, a lovely boy and a beautiful player. He had exquisite timing on the front or back foot, he scored more than 100 hundreds and made runs galore in county cricket, but could not cut it at Test match level. Why? The answer has to be between the ears. I don't know how true this is, but I heard that one time after he was dismissed in a Test match, he was in the toilets bashing his head against the door.

The contrast is David Steele. Watch him and you would call him an ugly duckling compared to Ramprakash. He mainly played on the front foot, had a dogged defence and was a tough nut to crack. He had limited ability but was up for the most difficult challenges, he stood up to Jeff Thomson and the West Indian quicks, Michael Holding, Andy Roberts and Wayne Daniel. You would love him in your team.

I once heard Jack Nicklaus, the great golfer, being interviewed. He was asked which was his favourite club to play with. He pointed to his head and said: 'The one between the ears.' He summed it up wonderfully. In an individual sport like golf or tennis, I can see that maybe the psychology side helps, but I do not see why England paid for a psychologist to come on tour up to the first Test.

If a player wants to see someone privately then fine, the ECB can sort out a session and pay for it. Today's players are programmed into following orders. When you are batting and bowling, you have to work things out for yourself or you ask your batting partner for advice; Broad and Anderson sometimes field at mid off when they are bowling together, so they can talk to each other. The best players ask questions and have an inquisitive mind. In the middle of a match, Plan A may not work so you need to be able to think quickly on your feet and try a Plan B. If that does not work, think quickly again and make a Plan C.

Good cricketers have to be able to adjust. But if you have been told what to do so often and programmed to follow orders from people, then you are in trouble. At the crease you can't pick up a telephone and speak to the coach, you need to use your brain and I was always taught a thinking cricketer is a better cricketer.

Andy organised every detail of the players' lives, thinking that would make England a better team. In other words, he took professionalism to the extreme. He may have preferred that when he played, but players are not computers. They are individuals in a team framework, each guy has to have space to be himself. It is up to the captain and coach to make sure he plays for the team. Mike Brearley was excellent at allowing individuality to thrive. The big phrase he used was: 'Is it really a big deal what the individual does if it does not harm the team ethos?'

In a team environment, laughter is important. It relaxes everybody, and when players are feeling good there is lots of banter and teams play better. It releases tension and stress. All you have to do as a captain is have lots of laughter in the morning, but 10–15 minutes before the start of play say: 'Right lads, let's switch on.'

Apparently when Darren Lehmann took over the Aussie set-up, he decided that each morning a different player would tell a funny story. You can imagine the ribbing a player gets if he tells a bad joke. I think when you have too much organisation and too many backroom staff you become a robot. The disciplined, work ethic is OK, but only to a point. If there is too much it becomes over-bearing, tedious and repetitive. Players become wooden tops waiting to be told what to do. They go through the motions and it is not enjoyable anymore. They do not look forward to playing cricket and their performances decline as a result. England's Ashes tour was a great example of that happening. By the end nobody could be excused for the way England played.

I was so unhappy with what I saw. There is no shame in being beaten, but it is the way you lose that counts. You have to fight to the end, but by the time of the fourth and fifth Tests in Melbourne and Sydney the England players were mentally shot. It was embarrassing; it looked as if they had given up. When Steve Waugh was captain of Australia he coined the phrase 'mental disintegration'. When a team is beaten in the head and they have given up on the prospect of winning, then it is all over. No amount of talent can make up for that mental state. That is exactly how we looked during the final two Tests.

Captains and coaches have a limited shelf life. You can only talk to people for so long before there is nothing new anymore. Players have heard it all before and the message goes in one ear and out the other. They are not really listening. Andy Flower had had some success, but he had reached the end of the road.

Soon after the Ashes series, he was told if he went quietly the ECB would find him a safe job. Two months later that safe job turned out to be titled 'Technical Director of Elite Coaching', with the focus on developing leadership skills and exploring technical innovation in coaching. It entails working with the next generation of England players and coaches, and he will also look to enhance the relationship between the county coaches and the England set-up.

All I can say is this is yet again another example of the ECB having more money than sense. They waste it by making up jobs and having more unnecessary backroom staff. One minute they cry out they need as much TV money as possible, then they throw it around like confetti. This would not be happening if ECB officials had to spend their own money. So, after the worst defeat England has ever suffered, not just in terms of the result but the embarrassing nature of the team's capitulation, we have the man who was in charge now teaching our future coaches and players how to do it. Do the ECB not see the irony in that?

It makes me fear for the future. The next generation of players will grow up not thinking for themselves. The new head coach of the England team, Peter Moores, has to address this and make the atmosphere more inclusive and less of a school classroom.

CHAPTER 11

KP THE ENIGMA

When England sacked Kevin Pietersen in the aftermath of the Ashes whitewash, the public were split. Many were mystified why the team's best player had been made a scapegoat when others had been more culpable for the thrashing by Australia, such as the captain Alastair Cook, the selectors and the coach Andy Flower.

Pietersen was England's highest runscorer in Australia, although that wasn't a particularly hard thing to achieve given their rotten performances, and a player who thrilled the public with some of his daring strokeplay. Many cricket lovers just wanted to see him bat and did not care about dressing-room politics. They paid their money and enjoyed being on edge when KP was at the crease. I know, because I loved watching him bat too. He could change a game in a flash. At the back of the mind was always the worry he would play a daft shot and get out, and for that reason nobody wanted to go to the toilet or to the bar while he was batting. Everybody watched with anticipation.

But it would be wrong to think Kevin was the sacrificial lamb for the Ashes whitewash. This massive decision by England was not taken with one series in mind. It was based on cricketing reasons and issues of discipline. In many ways England had only themselves to blame. They were too soft on him, allowing him to play stupid shots and throw his wicket away too many times without consequence. That came back to haunt them in Australia.

On other occasions, Kevin let himself down with his hubris and arrogance which culminated in the crisis of 2012, when he was caught texting his mates in the South African team. Alastair Cook fought hard to persuade the ECB to give Kevin another chance, but he lost patience with him a year later and was instrumental in sacking him.

The disconnect between Pietersen and the ECB began with his first sacking by England in 2009. The relationship never recovered. It changed the whole dynamic between star player and his employer. I felt for Kevin when he lost the captaincy. It was a messy, shameful period, dealt with in a ham-fisted way by our administrators.

Up to that point Pietersen had been a talented player who had not caused England any trouble, other than for his occasional hairstyles, and he had been managed well by a strong captain in Michael Vaughan. When Michael Vaughan resigned from the captaincy in August 2008, after the defeat at Edgbaston in the third Test of the series against South Africa, and Paul Collingwood, captain of the one-day team, also stood down, Kevin was made captain.

England wanted one leader across both major formats of the game, and he was the only player pretty much guaranteed his place in Test and one-day cricket so he got the job on that basis. There were reservations over whether his personality could stand the test of captaincy but they were ignored. They gambled. He started in typical Pietersen style, with a hundred in his first Test and a win over South Africa at The Oval.

But trouble was brewing. Pietersen had to work with Peter Moores, who had been appointed as head coach, replacing Duncan Fletcher in April 2007. The ECB rushed into his appointment, immediately promoting him from his job running the England Academy in Loughborough to be head coach of the senior side only a day after Fletcher resigned, and it was a disaster waiting to happen.

Pietersen's first tour as England captain was to India in 2008–09 and it was marred by the terrorist attacks in Mumbai. The England team left India and went to the UAE for a holding camp to decide whether or not to return to India. Pietersen was instrumental in persuading the players it would be safe to go back, winning a lot of goodwill in the process.

It was a strong stand to take, but the tour did not go well on the field and at the end of it Pietersen was asked for his thoughts on how to improve matters. It was at that point he suggested the sacking of Moores and his assistant, Andy Flower. In the case of Flower, it was a fateful call by Pietersen, who would spend the rest of his England career working under a man he had wanted sacked. After the tour to India, Pietersen spent Christmas and the New Year period on holiday with his family in South Africa.

Behind his back all hell was breaking loose as news of his

demands appeared in the *Daily Telegraph* on New Year's Eve. Pietersen looked arrogant because he was calling for the sacking of two senior coaches, even though he had been captain for only three matches. Both Moores and Flower had been appointed by the ECB and had strong backers higher up the command chain, yet here was Pietersen saying they were not good enough for the job. Kevin had misjudged the mood badly.

He expected to return to England at the end of his holiday to meet with Hugh Morris, then the managing director of the England team, to plan the future. But before he returned home, the ECB's executive board decided to sack Kevin and Moores. Somebody leaked that decision to the media and it became an absolute mess. Hugh was hoping to meet Kevin when he returned and tell him face-to-face he had been sacked, but because somebody could not keep their trap shut and leaked it, Morris realised it would be hugely difficult for KP when he arrived home for his meeting. The press would be waiting at the airport and he would be walking into an ambush. Morris tried to salvage the situation by telling KP over the phone he had lost his job.

It was a humiliating time for Pietersen. He had gone from asking for the coach to be removed, and believing he would have a say in the naming of his replacement, to being sacked over the phone himself. KP was persuaded to officially 'resign' in order to save himself from a great deal of embarrassment, but I am sure the hurt and pain of being dismissed never left him. It probably lingers even now and he will be bitter about it for the rest of his life. Once Kevin lost the captaincy, somebody had to grab him quickly and ensure his priorities were playing for England by giving him the opportunity to justify his talent, but suddenly he was an outsider as the team found a new spirit under Andrew Strauss and Flower.

Results improved and they won the Ashes that summer, a victory that looked impossible a few months earlier at the height of the Moores–Pietersen crisis. The turnaround vindicated the decision to sack KP and Moores. With Strauss's success in the role, Pietersen knew his chance of being captain again had gone.

Just a month after he was sacked as captain, Pietersen was bought by the Royal Challengers Bangalore for $1.55 million, opening the door to riches in the IPL. Now disaffected by English cricket, he knew he could earn vast sums of money playing in India for six weeks in Twenty20 where it doesn't matter if you get out playing a brainless shot. But the problem for Kevin was that international commitments cut his time in the IPL and impacted on how much money he could earn. His loyalty was split. Within a couple of years, matters came to a head.

Flower played a big part in this. The ECB had a retainer in Pietersen's central contract and could limit his time in the IPL. They wanted him back for the early home Test series in May, which clashed with the IPL. It meant Pietersen could play in the IPL for only three weeks, severely limiting how much money he could earn. It was a very uneasy compromise. KP wanted it all, but had forgotten that playing for England had helped him become a star. You can't have your cake and eat it. You cannot have a central contract, play in the juicy series against Australia, South Africa and India and yet skip other international cricket to play in the IPL. Real life does not work like that.

He wanted to play in a full IPL and then come back to play for England when it suited Kevin Pietersen. No employer would accept that in any job or profession. Finally the situation boiled over when KP announced his retirement from one-day cricket in the spring of 2012. He wanted to play only Twenty20s and Tests, but England would not allow that, saying that he could not pick and choose, but had to play all forms of one-day cricket or none at all, so he retired from one-day cricket.

It must have looked to his bosses at the ECB like childish behaviour. He was taking his bat home and sulking because they would not let him play in the IPL for as long as he wanted. Such a situation does not come to a head without plenty of meetings and discussions beforehand. It became wearying and irritating for England to have to spend so much time dealing with just one player, particularly as they had recently been beaten 3–0 by Pakistan and were planning for a series in the summer against South Africa that would decide which team was No.1 in the Test rankings.

Move on to Headingley in August of that year and he played a brilliant innings in the second Test against South Africa, scoring that fabulous 149 against the best seam attack in the world at the time. But then the story emerged he had been sending SMS messages that were apparently critical of Strauss and Flower to 'close friends' in the opposition dressing room. ECB officials were furious with him and many wanted him out forever. You just do not rubbish your captain to the opposition.

There is no excuse for that behaviour. If you are making derogatory comments about your two bosses to the opposition, it is traitorous. It always seemed that Pietersen said or did something silly when he felt his batting was unassailable.

Success went to his head. It was unheard-of in my day. We did not have mobile phones or the internet, of course, but they just provided Pietersen with the means to cause trouble.

The culture during my career was to keep everything within the dressing room. In the early 1960s at Yorkshire under Brian Close and in the 1970s playing for England with Mike Brearley as captain, we all had our say in the dressing room. You could have your moans and groans about anything – other players or tactics – and strong feelings were sometimes expressed. The captain took it all in, then made a decision and we all followed him; whether we thought he was right or wrong was then irrelevant. It did not matter because he was the boss. It certainly was not discussed outside the dressing room, it stayed in-house and was never revealed to our opponents.

We all knew deep down that if you betrayed that trust, the chairman of Yorkshire, Brian Sellers, would sack you. There were no employment laws or unfair dismissal actions in those days. You were out on your ear. I do not think the England selectors would have picked you again either, and we did not have central contracts with England to fall back on. You were invited by the TCCB to play one Test match at a time, so it was easy for the selectors to get rid of you whenever they wanted.

If England had sacked KP over the texting issue, nobody could have defended him. Michael Vaughan is a big supporter of Pietersen's, but he said: 'They could have moved him on and nobody would have batted an eyelid.' After weeks of meetings and speculation, England took him back. I know the chairman, Giles Clarke, other ECB officials and coach Flower did not want him back. Strauss was hurt, but he had resigned and left the scene.

Cook was the new captain and he was the one chiefly responsible for getting KP back in the team. Presumably he had wanted him because as a new captain he thought Pietersen would help him win matches and cement his position. Alastair must have believed he could get the best out of Kevin and build up a good relationship. When a captain wants a guy back, then he gets his way. Cricket puts great emphasis on the captain. He is the guy who leads the team for six hours a day in the field and makes all the big calls. When a captain stands up for a player, or the opposite and says he has to go, then he usually gets his own way.

For the Ashes tour of 1970–71, Ray Illingworth promised Basil D'Oliveira he would pick him in the squad. Illy had made the pledge earlier in the year after England's tour to South Africa in 1968–69 had been cancelled because the South African government refused to accept a squad which included Basil. When Raymond sat down to choose the squad for the Australia tour, various committee men did not want him in the team. Raymond said he had promised Dolly he would be in his squad, and if the selectors decided not to pick him then he could not go as captain, it would be breaking his word. Basil went to Australia and played in all six Tests.

In the end the buck stops with the captain. He has the most authority and Cook swayed the others, like Illy years before. Pietersen was reintegrated. It was an uneasy truce at first. Every movement KP made on the subsequent tour to India was scrutinised. I wrote at the time: 'A leopard does not change his spots.' Then KP played that wonderful innings in Mumbai. His 186 in the second Test was the best innings I saw him play for England, because for the first 70 runs he batted carefully and in an orthodox fashion on a turning pitch. At some point in the 70s he exploded and it was marvellous to watch. It turned the series and England went on to record a magnificent victory.

There was no more talk of Pietersen being a troublemaker. Matt Prior tweeted a picture in the Mumbai dressing room holding up a sign which said 'reintegration complete'. Cook's decision to bring him back looked vindicated, but I said to myself: 'Give it time.'

A year later and it was over. We cannot say for sure what went on in the England dressing room in Australia. We can only guess and speculate from bits of tittle-tattle we hear. Instead, we have to look at the facts. England lost badly and Pietersen played some awful shots as England paid the price for letting him bat in his own style for far too long. I was a supporter of his talent and I am honest enough to say I could never have played some of the innings he produced. But I also would not have played the irresponsible shots that often cost him his wicket.

He got away with playing the way he pleased for most of his career because England were winning. From time to time he made telling contributions with superb innings but any time he failed or played a silly shot, he would always absolve himself of any criticism by saying 'that is the way I play'. In other words, take it or leave it. That is OK for a while, when results are going your way, but it grates when the team is losing badly as they were in Australia. The silly shots were magnified and gave the impression he did not care and that the team's situation was not his problem.

I was critical of some of his poor shots in Australia; there were some absolute howlers. I called him a 'mug' and I stand by it now. With his team in trouble, he made some mind-boggling decisions. It started in the first Test at the Gabba. In the first innings Australia set the trap by stationing two short midwickets, KP took on the challenge and was caught clipping to one of those two fielders. In the second innings he fell for another sucker punch, hooking a short ball from Mitchell Johnson to long leg.

Then in Adelaide in the second Test he was again caught at midwicket exactly where Michael Clarke had put his fielders, it was stupid. My BBC *Test Match Special* colleague, Jonathan Agnew, summed it up well. 'We just want him to bat with responsibility,' he said. We wanted him to assess the position of the match and try to play accordingly. Even if he failed, and was bowled by a snorter or dismissed in some other fashion, then at least he would have been getting out playing for the team and the match situation. But too often he did not do that.

There was no excuse. Kevin played his 100th Test in Brisbane at the start of the Ashes series. He had been an international player for nearly a decade. You expect your senior, experienced players to give a lead, so it was either a case of he couldn't do it or wouldn't do it. But the worst was yet to come. In the second innings of the third Test at the WACA, with his team trying to save the game, he hit the off-spinner Nathan Lyon for six over long on. Australia dropped a man back on the boundary and Pietersen was caught trying to repeat the shot. It looked as if he did not give a damn that the Ashes were about to be lost.

What I know from having played international cricket and being in an England dressing room is that when one of your team-mates plays a howler of a shot there is a deathly silence. Then someone will spit out what you are all thinking and swear. Everyone is muttering: 'What the hell was that?' If it happens regularly, then I do not see how any captain or coach can criticise other batsmen for playing poor shots. How can they tell youngsters or new kids like Ben Stokes what is expected of them if a senior player like Pietersen is getting out in stupid ways? All the kids have to do is turn around and say: 'What about KP? He does what he wants and nobody says anything to him.'

My other point is if the captain and coach had admonished Kevin in the past, but he ignored them, then it was even worse behaviour on his part because he had clearly not listened. If that was the case then it was insubordination. Trust had broken down, which cannot be good for team unity and eventually it wears the management down. People get fed up and irritated and they start to think: 'Is it worth it? Do I want this problem anymore?' You start wondering if the pluses of having a player like KP in the team outweigh the negatives.

Pietersen mixed brilliant innings with irresponsible shots throughout his career. He was close to Vaughan, but let him down in his final Test. Vaughan was fighting to keep his job and Pietersen had a chance to set South Africa a tough last-innings target. But he got out on 94, trying to hit a six to bring up his hundred, England collapsed letting South Africa win and 48 hours later Vaughan had resigned.

On Flower's first tour in charge in the West Indies, incidentally Pietersen's first innings after losing the captaincy, he fell in identical fashion for 97 in Jamaica. He again tried to reach his hundred with a big six, this time off the left-arm spinner Sulieman Benn. His hubris got the better of him, because at that time people were just starting to talk about his habit of getting out to left-arm spinners, so he tried to show them he had no problem. Technically, I never thought he had an issue against left-arm spinners. He made it an issue by trying to bash them, to show us all he was not bothered by left-arm spin. His ego got him out, not his technique.

The daft shots in Australia were not the product of just one bad tour. It was a weakness that has stained his legacy as a batsman. You cannot argue against Pietersen being one of the best attacking batsmen in the modern era, but he will not be remembered as a great player because there were times when he couldn't or wouldn't grasp he should have played more for the needs of the team. Being cocky and confident with a touch of arrogance is part of the make-up of a great batsman, but too many times when the team needed him to play carefully, he let hubris get in the way of common sense. Once this happened time and again in Australia, the other baggage he brought with him began to weigh heavily on the management once again. When the tour ended, a meeting was held at Lord's to discuss Pietersen's future.

Flower had already stood down and he should not have had a say in Kevin Pietersen's future, but I am confident he will have been asked for his views. The only ones gathered for the actual meeting to discuss the Ashes tour were Paul Downton, the new managing director of the England team, James Whitaker, the new senior selector, and Alastair Cook. What is important to remember this time is that Cook must not have stood up for Kevin. We'd all heard a year previously how he had swayed opinion to bring Kevin back into the fold, and once again he had the power to wield a stay of execution, but presumably decided to let the axe fall.

There is no way Downton and Whitaker, both new to their jobs, would have gone against the England captain, particularly after it had been decided Cook could keep his job despite the 5–0 defeat. Alastair was very lucky to still be captain, partly because there was no obvious alternative, so in such a precarious situation he was not going to rock the boat by blaming the ECB or the management for the Ashes failure.

Kevin was different, though; he had no friends at the ECB. There would be no point keeping Cook as captain and then ignoring him if he said Pietersen should stay in the side. A couple of weeks earlier, Ashley Giles, the coach of the one-day and Twenty20 team and selector, had stated Pietersen was a 'million-pound asset' when he was asked about his team for the Twenty20 World Cup in Bangladesh. As soon as Flower stood down as coach, Giles went on record to say he wanted the head coach's job. If he had really wanted KP in the World Twenty20 team you would think he would have made his feelings known to the new managing director and chairman of selectors. But Giles can't have been very persuasive or he was talked around to the others' views. If Cook and Giles had been strong about retaining Pietersen, he would have survived but they abandoned him and he had played his last innings for England.

If Michael Vaughan had been captain throughout Pietersen's career, he would have managed him better and been strong enough to nip any problems in the bud, but Strauss, Giles and Cook are all mild-mannered and soft-natured people. They indulged him for a quiet life, because of his match-winning talent, and were never going to handle KP firmly in a million years. They allowed him to do his own thing on the field and play his own way with no discipline. The situation snowballed and was bound to end in tears.

When it did it was a nasty time for English cricket, as Pietersen's friends mounted a public-relations campaign against the ECB, who were slow to react. It was led by Piers Morgan, the former editor of the *Daily Mirror*, who is a friend, confidant and admirer of KP, but I don't think he did the lad any favours by tweeting comments and making statements supporting him and criticising the cricketing authorities. Piers, like anyone else, is entitled to his opinion and to give his views, but because he was known to be so close to Kevin, it gave the impression that KP was feeding him information and Piers was his mouthpiece.

I had a similar situation happen to me in the winter of 1983–84 when Yorkshire sacked me as a player. A known supporter and close friend of mine at the time, Sydney Fielden, was trying to be my mouthpiece and, because he was so close to me and shared my company, he knew many private and confidential matters. Unbeknown to me, he was speaking to the Yorkshire committee and the media and anyone else who would listen, giving the impression his words were coming from me. I only learned of it later and discovered how it had put the backs up of some members of our committee. People like Syd and Piers think they are helping you, but it can be counterproductive, and I think this is what happened with KP and the ECB.

Kevin was restricted in what he could say, due to him being under contract to the ECB, and rightly or wrongly people got the impression that this was Kevin's way of getting around it, particularly when tweets emerged criticising Matt Prior. The two men had clearly fallen out, but conducting a public spat on

Twitter did little for Pietersen's cause. Nasser Hussain summed up Pietersen astutely after his final sacking: 'History tells you with Kevin that he hasn't really got a foot to stand on whether it be back in Natal; or Hampshire or Nottinghamshire; whether it be Peter Moores or Andrew Strauss or Alastair Cook or Andy Flower – wherever he's been he's been a problem.'

Some believe in cutting out the virus and moving on while others say you should just man-manage your best players. But the people running England were fed up with dealing with Pietersen and could not handle him any longer. They looked at everything that had gone on in the past and decided the previous five years since the captaincy issue had been characterised by too many meetings and acrimony around Kevin.

What he wanted and what he did took up too much time. People put up with it when the team was winning and KP was batting well, but against Australia in England in 2013 he averaged 38.80 and 29.40 in the return series. Some will say those figures are better than most of the others, but England needed more from a player as good as Pietersen to justify all the aggravation he caused. In the end, he was not worth the bother if he was producing figures that were comparable with the rest. England were humiliated in Australia and heads had to roll. Jonathan Trott and Graeme Swann had gone before the tour reached the fourth Test and Flower later resigned.

There was a new team to be formed under a new coach and, having decided Cook would stay, it was time for a fresh start and they did not want to rebuild the team around younger players while worrying if Pietersen would be a malign influence on impressionable young cricketers. It was time to move on.

Pietersen has always been charming when our paths have

crossed and he speaks well about cricket in the media. He has never been caught up in an off-field scandal involving booze or fighting. He is a consummate professional in the way he prepares for matches and works on his fitness. He always signed autographs for kids and even posed for pictures with fans while fielding on the boundary, but clearly there are deeper issues.

The late Tony Greig wrote that there were similarities between myself and KP in that we were both mavericks and unusual individuals. Things certainly seemed to be always happening around us, like when we both briefly held the captaincy of England. He had the distraction of the terrorist attacks in Mumbai and I had the Pakistan Packer players' dispute in Karachi. Instead of being able to concentrate on the captaincy and the cricket, the other issues become all-encompassing. It is a nightmare trying to juggle the players' and the ECB's wishes. Also, our wicket was always the most prized by the opposition bowlers and the media always knew they would have a story if they could get our name in the headlines. We both had a name that captured the imagination, and always being in the headlines for cricket or other things can cause jealousy from other players.

The oddest thing is, for different types of players in different eras, our Test records are almost the same. Pietersen played 104 Tests, scored 8,181 runs at an average of 47.28 with 23 hundreds. I played 108 Tests, hit 8,114 runs at 47.72 with 22 hundreds, but I never slagged off my captain or team-mates to the opposition while playing with them. When it was put to Mike Gatting in Melbourne during the Ashes tour that KP and Geoffrey Boycott were the same he replied: 'Both like batting and know their averages, but Geoffrey never gave his wicket away and wanted England to win. Kevin gives his wicket away and is indifferent to England winning.' England never lost a Test match when I made a century.

Pietersen was sacked at 33, and still has cricket left in him before he retires. He will make more money than anyone currently in world cricket. KP will be rubbing shoulders with superstars of Indian cricket who earn many millions from their IPL contracts and endorsements. He will be ranked alongside the likes of Mahendra Singh Dhoni, the current Indian and World Cup-winning captain, who earns more money than any other cricketer.

Now KP is available to play the whole of the IPL, he will be able to receive his full fee as he can now stay for the duration of the tournament. He will have immense 'pulling power' and be a target for product association and a brand ambassador. He is also free to 'have bat, will travel' and play all the Twenty20 cricket competitions around the globe. He can have the choice of the 'Big Bash' in Australia around the Christmas and New Year holiday period or the South African Twenty20 series called the 'Ram-Slam' tournament in January and February. He has a deal with Surrey and, if the dates are right, he could in future fit in the Caribbean Premier League. There is a Twenty20 in Bangladesh, although they may have to pay him a fortune to go out there.

He will get astronomical sums for a 'kiss and tell' book due out later this year in which he is sure to settle scores with old team-mates, the ECB and the media. He will give his side of what went on with Flower, Strauss and Cook. Financially he is going to be so much better off than if he'd had his wish and stayed on playing cricket for England in the hope of scoring

10,000 Test runs, as he was quoted as saying. Television stations will be keen to have him commentate on any England matches, it will catch the imagination of the public and media. He will be in demand and become very wealthy.

The bitterness over England will remain, but Pietersen's career will go down as proof that you can be an individual in a team, but you can't just be an individual because it is a team game. It is that simple.

CHAPTER 12

PLOTTING
A WAY BACK

If England are to have any chance of reclaiming the Ashes in 2015, they have to nullify the threat and impact of Mitchell Johnson by being a lot smarter to reduce his wicket-taking ability. If our batsmen try to take him on then there will only be one winner and it will not be Alastair Cook and his mates. No team in the history of cricket has won the war against genuine fast bowling by going toe-to-toe with the quicks. History shows that occasionally a batsman will play a fantastic innings – one that takes your breath away and is thrilling and memorable to watch – but they do not win the Test series for his team.

In the first Test of the Bodyline series of 1932–33 at Sydney, Stan McCabe hooked his way to 187 not out, but it was a fleeting success against Larwood and Voce as England still won by ten wickets. You can always guarantee that at some stage in a series, the big fast bowler will dominate and he will win a couple of matches.

During the Ashes series of 1974–75, in the first Test at Brisbane, Tony Greig scored 110 for England against Lillee and Thomson, but they still lost. In the series Lillee and Thomson took 57 wickets between them in the first five Tests and Australia easily won four, with one drawn. In the sixth Test match at Melbourne, Thomson was injured and did not play. Lillee broke down, bruising his right foot and left the field after bowling only six overs. As a consequence, Australia were without any fast bowlers and England won their only Test match of the series, with Mike Denness and Keith Fletcher scoring centuries.

In 1976 when England played the West Indies at The Oval, Dennis Amiss had been struggling against fast bowling and been left out of the first four matches. He made a fantastic 203 against Andy Roberts, Michael Holding and Wayne Daniel, but England still lost the match by 231 runs. Most people remember this match because Michael Holding took eight wickets for 92 runs and six for 57 on one of the flattest pitches of all time.

Allan Lamb was an excellent player of fast bowling, and in 1984 versus the West Indies he made 110, 100 and 100 not out in consecutive Test matches at Lord's, Leeds and Old Trafford, yet England still lost all three matches badly to the fast bowling of Joel Garner, Malcolm Marshall and Michael Holding.

And finally, Kevin Pietersen made a superb century against South Africa at Headingley in 2012. At the time, they had the best fast bowling attack in the world and the match was drawn, but England still lost the series 2–0. So you see, fleeting brilliance with the bat thrills and entertains at the time, but it normally only delays the inevitable.

It is possible Mitchell Johnson will be injured and unable to play next year. He could revert back to his old ways of spraying the ball all over the place, but I think that is highly unlikely. He has found such confidence and a way to be aggressive, bowl fast and take wickets, so England have to plan for him being fit and in form. They have to find a way of combating him; it does not matter if we do not score off him, but we can't afford him taking another 37 wickets at 13 each. If he does then the Ashes series will be over before it starts.

If I remember rightly, a Test match lasts five days, although you wouldn't know it by watching us in Australia. During the last Ashes series, the Tests in Brisbane and Melbourne finished in four days, Sydney in three days, Adelaide one hour into the fifth day and Perth finished at lunch time on the last day. Scoring quickly is lovely, but when you are not able to do that then it is better to score slowly than not at all. It falls to all the batsmen to improve. The England batsmen have to learn to be more patient and keep their wickets intact, exhaust Johnson and make him work harder by bowling a lot of overs for little reward. They need to plan, prepare and above all execute better.

England's batting succumbed too easily and too quickly in Australia, meaning the opposition bowlers were never tired but the England bowlers did not get the same chance to put their feet up, because before long they were strapping their boots on and were out there bowling again. It was a complete contrast to three years previously, when England's batsmen made high scores, giving their bowlers lots of rest. They need to get back to that scenario.

With back-to-back Test matches, it is exhausting for a bowler if he does not have enough rest so it is imperative to keep the Australians in the field for longer by posting decent totals. The England batsmen have to understand they need to get smarter, they have to box clever like Muhammad Ali against George Foreman in 1974. Foreman had knocked out 37 of his 40 opponents before he took on Ali. He was world champion, much bigger and stronger than Ali and punched harder. Ali realised there would be no point trying to slug it out with Foreman, it would be a no-win situation. It is exactly what I am saying here with Johnson, they need to adapt to the situation.

Ali always had fast hands and quick feet but he could not out-punch George, so what did he do? He did his homework and realised this big heavy man had never gone more than a few rounds because he had always knocked his opponents out early in his fights. So Ali thought he would tire him out by staying on the ropes, letting George throw punches that kept hitting his arms which eventually exhausted Foreman. Then Ali took his chance and knocked him out, afterwards they coined it 'Rope a Dope'.

The new England head coach, Peter Moores, needs to impress on his batsmen a better strategy is needed, rather than playing virtually a shot a ball against Johnson. Not only is a plan needed, but it then has to be implemented well. Occasionally a guy like Johnson will bowl on a slow pitch that takes the sting out of his bowling, but that happens infrequently now in modern-day Test matches. The technology and know-how about preparing pitches have improved beyond recognition. We can't just produce slow, low pitches to nobble Johnson. The test for England is to sort the problem a different way.

I know the World Cup is before the Ashes and England have

never won it. It would be tremendous to win it this time, but which is the bigger prize? Is it winning the World Cup in March of 2015 or beating Australia and getting the Ashes back? Ask fans which they would prefer, yes we would like to win both, but the Ashes are the jewel in the crown. They always have been and hopefully always will be.

Alastair Cook needs to keep in mind that winning generals take all the honours and are feted, but losing generals get the sack, and he was lucky to retain his job after the shambolic Ashes tour. In order for him to keep the captaincy, he and his batsmen have to get back to scoring totals of more than 400 in the first innings of every game. It is not absolutely vital to score 500, but 400 runs puts them in a position of strength from which they can then have a big say in the course of the game.

Even if the opposition also goes on to make a big total, there is still more chance of saving the match. It usually takes up three days for two teams to score around 900 runs, leaving only two days for a further two innings. Whether you win or lose the toss, you will not be beaten very often if you score totals of more than 400 in your first innings.

Bowlers love it when their batsmen have put runs on the board. Ask any bowler, if the batsmen have given them a platform to work with they are more relaxed so bowl better. It is amazing then how much scoreboard pressure is put on the opposition. But make low totals then you will be the team under pressure all the time, tensions creep in and the other side get a sniff of victory.

Our England batsmen need to get back to basics and get rid of all these one-day shots: reverse sweeps, scoops and paddles. It is madness to be playing them in a Test match. In the first innings of the second Test match in Adelaide last winter, Joe Root, batting at No.3, got out for 15 playing a scoop shot off the off-spinner Nathan Lyon. Why did he think he needed to play a scoop? There was plenty of time left in the Test and England needed to build an innings. They were facing an Australian total of 570 for nine declared and the pitch was good for batting. It was crazy.

Hooking is another shot fraught with danger, pulling is a much better per centage stroke. When the ball bounces chest high, it is much easier to control it playing a pull. Once the ball gets throat and head high, it is harder to keep down. We have all made the mistake of hooking those balls, myself included. You can make that mistake once, but you can also make sure you don't do it again.

When I used to play against West Indian Malcolm Marshall, the greatest fast bowler ever, he would see me in the car park before the game and, with a big smile on his face, shout: 'Are you hooking today, Boycs?' and I would shout back: 'Not if you're bowling.'

In February 2014 in the second Test at Port Elizabeth, the South Africans showed how to bat against Mitchell Johnson. In the first Test at Centurion, he had blown them away. Graeme Smith was out hooking, players were hit on the head, and too many played indiscriminate shots. It was as if they hadn't watched the Ashes series. They were taken by surprise and Johnson took 12 wickets in the match.

South Africa then did their homework and, unlike England in the previous Ashes series, they occupied the crease, batted slowly with care and a lot of patience to make a total of 423 runs. They took Johnson out of the equation and he got one for

70 in the first innings and two for 51 in the second. It may not have been spectacular batting, but it worked, and by taking the time to put a good total on the board they won the match. The South Africans realised that if Johnson takes a bag-full of wickets at a low cost against you, there is no way you can win a Test match; you have to play him out of the game.

God knows how any of the modern batting teams would have got on against the West Indian quicks in the 1970s and 80s when there were four of them coming at you all day long and there was no respite. Sadly, I think too many of them would rely on sledging to try to talk their way out of trouble, which would be a recipe for disaster. I hope Peter Moores improves standards of behaviour on the field and doesn't sink to Australia's level next year. England should be the first to set their own standards and cut out the lip.

They need to be bigger than the other teams, let the verbals go over their heads and concentrate on playing well. That would wind the Aussies up more than anything else. It will take a lot for that to happen, because England have lost experienced players who could show a lead. Andrew Strauss, Kevin Pietersen and Jonathan Trott have all gone, leaving a more callow team but also a vulnerable batting line-up. There is time for that to change, but the selectors have to show some decisiveness and give new players a chance.

They have four series scheduled between the Ashes contests, but that involves only 12 Test matches (seven of which will have been played by the time this book is published) so it is important the selectors do their job well, identify guys who they think will make Test match players and then give them the opportunity to play in all 12 Test matches to gain as much experience as possible. It will be crucial who the selectors choose.

Losing KP and Trott has left a huge hole in the middle order. If Jonathan makes runs for Warwickshire, can England resist the temptation to bring him back into the team? He was a fine player with a good Test record but what if he returns, the pressure gets to him and he has to go home ill again? England would look like chumps. They say they have managed him once, but it will be risky to try it a second time. Five months after leaving the Ashes tour he gave an interview to Sky, and blamed his breakdown in Australia on 'burn out'. But he collapsed again after just one match for Warwickshire and I can't see how England can trust him again in the heat of Test cricket. If he gets back into the England team and plays the same amount of cricket again, how will he deal with all that travel and playing? Will the stress come back again? Will he run away again?

Those are the serious questions I would ask if I was a selector. Also, did he rush back to play county cricket because Warwickshire had given him a benefit and he knew if he played it would help swell his fund? Or was he just kidding himself? The boy had tears in his eyes at times during that Sky interview. It was all very raw for him. If he faces the Aussies again, they will not be shy with their onfield comments; in other words he will get plenty of sledging.

Jonathan Trott didn't play Johnson well in the ODIs in 2013, and in the first and only Test he faced him, Johnson dismissed him both times for 10 and 9. Anybody can fail, but in the 28 balls he received he looked very uncomfortable. He has always shuffled across the crease, but I noticed when playing Johnson he was shuffling across the crease and moving forward *before* Johnson had let the ball go. That's OK until the bowler bangs it in short of a length, gets lift like Johnson does and because of his pace the batsman has not got enough time to transfer his weight onto the back foot. If you are coming forward to a speed merchant before he delivers the ball, his eyes will light up and you are asking for one or two in the mouth. That's what he got and he was in trouble. It's vital to stay back until the bowler has let the ball go, only then should you decide to come forward or go further back.

Trott's absence means Ian Bell should move up to No.3. If he stays down the order, England will have to have a new inexperienced batsman at No.3 as well as a likely new opening partner for Cook, given Carberry's struggles in Australia. Facing the new ball with two unproven guys is very chancy. If Bell goes to bat at three, then he has to knuckle down and cut out the mistakes; somebody has to be firm with him, because it is not how quickly he scores or how dashing he looks at the crease, it is how many runs he makes. He must battle through the difficult periods with some patience rather than taking the bowlers on or trying to smack spinners over the top.

When bowlers are having a good period, he has to play through it and cannot always attack; he has to show a lot more maturity now Pietersen is out of the frame. Joe Root has been up and down the batting order since he came in the team, so England could finally give him a settled spot at No.4. The kid has immense talent and the character to be a top batsman for England for many years.

I do not think he is ready for opening the innings. I tried to tell various people, the selectors and the ECB, that he was not ready to open against high-quality bowling. I had watched him at Yorkshire in 2011 and 2012, and I spotted he had a bit to learn early on in his innings with his footwork against the new ball. He struggled getting his feet moving. If he gets in, he makes hundreds and looks terrific, but England did not listen.

The sudden departure of Andrew Strauss, retiring earlier than expected, left England with a big hole to fill at the top of the order and they were desperate for an opening batsman. England got sucked in to believing that because he scored runs for the Lions he was a ready-made opening batsman. He may well be one day, but it takes time. Test cricket has better and faster bowlers with a new ball in their hand and they are far more dangerous than county bowlers. When he opened in 2013 against Australia in England, he made one half century and a big hundred at Lord's after he was dropped on 8. In total, he had seven failures. That is not a good return for an opening batsman. If Australia had caught him when he was still in single figures at Lord's before he went on to score 180 it would have looked a lot worse.

The other problem is England fell in love with him to the point where they were picking him in all forms of the game. Wow! You would think we had Brian Lara and Sachin Tendulkar all rolled into one. In my opinion, picking him in all forms of the game has not helped his development. As a lovely, technically correct batsman can you see him as a Twenty20 crash-bang-wallop merchant? I can't. Slogging? Cross-batted shots? Using brute force to hit boundaries? Sorry, I do not see Joe Root as that kind of player. Not now, not ever. I believe this was misguided.

I watched him on television playing in a Twenty20 against

Australia in Melbourne. He came in, played a cover drive, one off his legs and then had a big slog and the ball went up in the air to backward point. How does that help the development of a 23-year-old kid? Many of the best Twenty20 players in the world are average Test match cricketers. Look at Kieron Pollard. He hits it everywhere in a Twenty20 game, but does not get picked in Test cricket for the West Indies, because he does not have the defence, technique or patience required.

Twenty20 is slog cricket and entertainment, but it is not the best preparation for an orthodox young batsman trying to learn how to build an innings. There are very few technically correct batsmen who do reasonably well in Twenty20, because T20 is not about orthodox batting. The few who have done well in Twenty20 playing orthodox shots are a lot older than Joe and have learnt their trade. They have been very successful over a number of years and understand their game. The best example is Mahela Jayawardena, the Sri Lankan batsman, who is magnificent in Test cricket but was able to transfer that to other forms of the game. In T20 you have to hit every ball for runs and it breeds bad habits for Test cricket, so that you then start doing it in any form of cricket without thinking.

As a young kid, Joe should be allowed to develop his game without the pressure of having to strike boundaries. England should get him back to playing orthodox cricket, because it is possible he could be as good in Test cricket as Jayawardena. At the moment, having a regular spot down the order where he can start his innings away from the new ball, is the ideal position for him. Given time, Joe will probably move up to open the innings, but leave the lad alone for now, let him develop.

Matt Prior should be our wicketkeeper in the next Ashes

series. He is a wonderful player and he has always been a positive influence batting down at No.7. But in 2013 his strength was his weakness. He tried to play shots, get on top of the bowlers before he got himself in. Now he is a very senior player and he has to show, like Bell, a bit more patience and common sense. The youngsters will be looking to Bell and Prior for guidance.

The batting coach has to work hard with our tailenders, because in Australia they were hopeless. All tailenders like playing medium pacers and spinners, because there is no physical danger, but however good they are at that, they are all shit-scared of fast bowling. The fear of facing Johnson just blew their minds before they reached the middle. They are not expected to score runs, but there is an expectation they will make Johnson and other bowlers spend lots of energy and effort on getting them out. Psychologically, Johnson's presence had damned them before they entered the arena. That is the fear of getting hurt and they need help in order to conquer it.

The coaches need to teach them how to defend and that should not be too difficult, because in the last 30 years everyone has been wearing a helmet with a grille, chest pad and an armguard, which reduces the chances of getting hurt. But if you stand there frightened of being hit, then you have no chance of staying in. They might as well not bother going out to the middle, because in Australia it was embarrassing. The Aussies rolled over the tail so quickly that it gave them a huge psychological lift.

Monty Panesar has to be our spinner. I don't have any doubt in my mind that he is our best spin bowler now Graeme Swann has retired. The worry for me is that Cook does not know how to manage Monty. He is a guy who thrives on confidence. It is going to be a test of Cook's man-management skills as captain to get the best out of Monty. He has to make Monty believe he wants him in the team.

Alastair gave me the impression in Australia that he did not trust Monty's bowling and there were times when I thought he should have bowled more in the two Tests he played in Adelaide and Melbourne. Instead, the captain threw the ball to someone else. England then dropped him in Sydney for Scott Borthwick, the young leggie who is not even a frontline spinner for his county Durham, but just happened to be out in Australia playing club cricket. Now if Monty gets an inkling that the captain does not believe in him, then he crumbles. It is an absolute must that Cook shows Monty he loves him and makes him feel fantastic. No negative vibes whatsoever or you lose him as a bowler.

Shane Warne will be negative about Monty to help his own Australian side and say he has played so many Tests for England but bowls with the same pace and same trajectory every time. I don't give a toss about what an Aussie says; forget any criticism and focus on the facts: he has taken over 150 Test wickets and helped England win matches.

Perhaps a young kid will emerge to displace Monty, but the next Ashes series will be a harsh environment for a spinner. We know Darren Lehmann, Michael Clarke and his team will use the same tactic as they did against Swann. All the batsmen will go after whoever is the spinner and try to knock him out of the attack. A young player could crumble under such pressure, but Monty has been in the situation before.

It looks as if England have unearthed a talented all-rounder in Ben Stokes. He has pace with the ball plus some ability with the bat, but England have to play him in every Test match now to gain experience. He has a lot to learn. He is still raw with the bat: he scored a good hundred in the second innings of the third Ashes Test at Perth, but then in Melbourne when we were trying to save the game he was caught at mid off trying to hit Nathan Lyon over the top on 19. That is when a coach has to get hold of him and say: 'OK, you got a hundred in Perth playing shots like that when you had seventy, but it is not a smart shot to be playing when we are trying to save the game.' That is the learning process which comes about from playing Test matches and talking to more senior people.

As with Joe Root, I would prefer to see him not playing in the Twenty20 format and be allowed to develop his cricket in Test matches and 50-over games only. These kids have no time to breathe, to collect themselves and take it all in. They play every minute at the top level living in a 'goldfish bowl' with no respite. Each of the three formats demands a different way of playing, a different understanding of what is needed and I think it is just too much to ask them to assimilate all that. England want them to run before they can walk, but their development needs to be paced. It is no surprise to me when these youngsters cannot maintain a high level of performance. The frustrations creep in.

On England's tour to the West Indies in March 2014, Ben had five failures with the bat. The frustration boiled over and he ended up breaking his wrist after punching a locker in the dressing room following a first-ball dismissal. A young player's development is like snakes and ladders. Up the ladder and down the snake, it's a roller coaster ride. Nowadays television makes young cricketers instantly famous, money comes pouring in, and they think they have made it. The adrenalin and testosterone is pumping. It is a fantastic, but also a difficult time in their career.

Good coaches should understand that young players' performances will go up and down and their emotions will fluctuate. It's a natural learning curve, so it is up to the coach to occasionally take them out of the spotlight for a break. Stokes can be a handy back-up bowler next summer, but England's main strikeforce should revolve around Steven Finn, who will hopefully be back to his best, and Stuart Broad. Jimmy Anderson and Graham Onions will be crucial swinging the ball and Chris Jordan from Sussex has pace. There is always room for somebody with genuine pace and Liam Plunkett might come into the reckoning.

Anderson has been our best bowler for years, playing in all formats of the game. As he gets older – he will be 33 during the next Ashes series – there is a need to keep him fresh and lessen his workload. He has been bowling for a long time and played a lot of cricket after more than 12 years at the top. It would be wise now to retire him from all forms of one-day cricket and save him for Tests only. He can still produce marvellous deliveries; the ball he bowled at Trent Bridge to Michael Clarke in the first Ashes Test of 2013 was a beauty. He brought Clarke forward, beat the bat and hit the top of off stump. Honestly, if he had bowled that to me ten times, he would have got me out ten times, although I would like to think I'd have nicked it and not missed it like Clarke! If Anderson can bowl balls like that, then you want him as fresh as a daisy, not travelling around the world playing one-day cricket.

On English pitches with the Duke ball, Onions can be very dangerous. I don't know why England ignored him in 2013, as he had fantastic figures for Durham, but for some reason they did not trust him. They have Onions and Anderson for swing, Broad and Finn for seam but they need some pace. Chris Jordan is young, raw and worth a punt, because young bowlers can develop very quickly and I was delighted that our selectors took a chance and gave him a few Test matches.

For me, Tim Bresnan is not a match-winning bowler in Test cricket and I would play him only in one-dayers. He is a good, strong guy and he will bowl a lot of overs. I can see why Flower and Cook liked him, but I prefer wicket-taking bowlers like Liam Plunkett, as they win Test matches.

Stuart Broad is a superb cricketer and was our best bowler in Australia. He has a big heart and the stomach for a fight, but you want him ready and fresh. He has had problems with injuries in the past and this will only get worse as he ages, so the selectors have to manage his workload carefully. It is a problem resting bowlers and keeping them fresh, but you cannot win every series and every World Cup by playing the same players. It is impossible. If you want them to be fit and ready for the Ashes, then you have to rotate and give bowlers time off.

Modern international teams have become like Premier League football clubs in recent years, they play so much we need large squads. Slowly and surely we are now seeing crick-eters being rested. There is a need to prioritise with most players and decide what is their best format. For example, Broad is the Twenty20 captain, a major player in 50 overs and Test matches, but while he might want to, it is not good for him to play every match. He will be knackered and pick up an injury. There is so much international cricket it is becoming a real problem for selectors to juggle players around.

England's run-up to the 2015 Ashes is a trip to Sri Lanka in November and December, where it is hot and hard for quick bowlers, a one-day tri-series in Australia in January and February, then the World Cup in Australia and New Zealand followed by three Tests in the West Indies in April before the English summer of two Test matches against New Zealand and then the Ashes.

They are going to have to manage resources very cleverly to keep our key guys fresh and fit for facing Australia. If they try to win every match and series with the same players, it will blow up in their faces. Yes, it is good to win, but for that to happen they will have to move players around. That takes skilful management and the one area of genuine worry for me is the leadership of Alastair Cook.

He is not the type of guy to criticise a player and tell him off, but occasionally as captain, he is going to have to face up to players. He has to show them he is the boss and not just because someone has given him some stripes to pin on his arm. That alone does not make you a leader. Leadership is about gaining the respect, trust and confidence of the rest of the team. Nobody can teach that; it comes naturally. There is no captaincy textbook or school.

You learn by watching others while growing up and asking questions of your elders. But even that is not enough, it is instinct; you have to feel the nuances of the game as they happen. It is about the ability to see an opportunity before it happens and to be strong enough to act rather than prevaricate or be too cautious. A lot of ex-players feel Cook's major problem is that he is too pedestrian, he waits too long before making his move and he follows the ball with his field placings. You have to be two steps ahead of the game in your thinking and I don't think Cook will ever get it. He is a nice lad and a top batsman and he will always be just that. He is not a gifted leader.

OK, Alastair had a dip in form in Australia, but that has happened to all of us and his runscoring will return. But the problem for Cook is that he will always be compared to his Australian opposite number, Clarke, who is very sharp. I accept people say: 'If not Cook, then who?' A lack of alternatives is a bigger problem for England to solve. But one day if Cook does not grasp it, then someone else will come on the scene and they will be made captain. You can't stick with a captain because he is a nice lad and a good batsman. He was lucky to survive the 5–0 in Australia, but the ECB realised they did not have anyone else to turn to. The only other candidate was Bell and he thinks even slower than Cook.

The best captain I played under was Ray Illingworth. If he saw an opportunity, he would move fast. What helped was that Raymond played a lot of his career on uncovered pitches, so he grew up expecting the unexpected. We played two three-day matches a week and every pitch was different. Then, if it rained on the pitch, it changed in character so you had to adapt to new conditions. Captains had to think ahead of the game. We also had to fit four innings in to three days, so time was always your enemy and you had to be smart to get results.

Perhaps we were lucky to grow up in an era when we had to think on our feet. But the modern-day player does not understand the challenges we faced. They think if you play on a pitch that has been rained on, the ball would fly past your head but that was not the case. It would seam, swing and turn on some days. On other occasions after rain it would do nothing, the ball would go straight and keep low so captains had to be good at judging situations. You had to keep a sharp brain all the time. Cook lets the game drift and rarely shows any imagination.

England may have the players to beat Australia, it is just whether they have the brains to go with the talent. Beating Australia is what the public demands. If we play as badly at home as we did in Australia and lose abjectly 5–0, there will be the biggest outcry cricket has ever seen from the public and the media. All hell will break loose. There will be a lot more losing their jobs than just Andy Flower, Kevin Pietersen and Graham Gooch. It will be an intriguing series.

ACKNOWLEDGEMENTS

A special thank you to my wife, Rachael, who has been very influential in how this book has turned out. She was my sub-editor throughout, checking my copy, providing advice and utilising her excellent memory to ensure my recollections are honest. Without her care and attention to detail, I could not have accurately recalled my difficulty with cancer, which forms an emotional part of this book.

Thank you Rachael, you were brilliant.

INDEX

(the initials GB refer to Geoffrey Boycott)